Pı

MW01702008

"Dan Blanchard's book is AMAZING and SO IMPORTANT!! His knowledge, wisdom, and belief in teens will help many lives!! His words and insight will also be utilized as a tool to help mold, shape, and guide teens—myself included—for the rest of our lives!

Julie Ann McCormick,
Hartford, Connecticut

"Feeling Lucky? is a must read for any family dealing with generational issues. A Grandfather reaches out to a troubled teen and helps him discover how to make it though turbulent times. The message of "Constant and Never-ending Deliberate Improvement" will help young and old to learn what it takes to succeed in an imperfect world. You will be "Feeling Lucky" after you read this book!"

January Jones, Blog Talk Radio host
and author of: *Thou Shalt Not Whine*
and *The Eleventh Commandment*

"Feeling Lucky? contains excellent common sense advice in a very easy read. I would recommend it to teenagers, parents, or anyone who works with young people."

Michael Foran
National Principal of the Year

"A must read for today's young adults! What a privilege to have an expert educator provide so much insight and inspiration through a modern story that really resonates with the tumultuous life of today's teens. This book will make a wonderful gift for any teen you wish to see succeed."

Krista H. Wells, Ph.D.,
Professional Speaker,
Military Spouse Coach

"It's rare these days to find a truly positive young adult text that is void of violence, sex, and drugs. Granddaddy's Secrets encompasses a great message while still being relevant to today's teens."

Colleen Moffett
Teacher of the Year

"If you're a teenager who could use a better role model, this book is for you, as the secrets of life are revealed to a teenager by his Granddaddy. It should also be read by teachers in the classroom, parents during family time, mentors who do one-on-one mentoring, and leaders who seek to develop those they lead. Not only is this a great story, but it is told by a great leader and mentor whom I greatly admire."

Dr. Richard M. Pfohl, CEO and
Founder of Navigos

Feeling Lucky?

Feeling Lucky?

by

Dan Blanchard

TLP

New Britain, Connecticut

Feeling Lucky?

Cover Illustrator: Emily Mann
Editor: Valerie Utton
Published by: Teen Leadership Publishing

www.GranddaddysSecrets.com

ISBN 10: 0986239801
ISBN 13: 978-0-9862398-0-9

Printed in the United States of America

Acknowledgements

A special thanks to my beautiful wife Jennifer, and our five precious children: Kalaiya, Dakota, Savanna, Aliya, and Seanna. They were all extremely patient with the many hours it took to create this book.

A special thanks to my editor, Valerie Utton, who always has great advice and plenty of thought provoking questions to ask.

Thank you to all the students I've had the pleasure of meeting over the years. You inspired me to write this book.

Further gratitude goes to our free public libraries. Even after all these years, I continue to learn from the books I find there.

Lastly, thank you to all the people, family, and friends who have inspired and supported me on this journey.

Sincerely,

Daniel R. Blanchard

Contents

Too many people waste their lives waiting for their lucky break. What they fail to realize is that luck isn't something you can wait for.

"Luck is when preparation meets opportunity."

Seneca

1

The Smell of Rain

"Out of difficulties grow miracles."

- Jean De La Bruyere

"I smell the coming of rain," Granddaddy said as we walked through the park on this cool breezy fall day.

I gave him a sideways look thinking how weird his statement was and couldn't help but notice Granddaddy was still in pretty good shape for an old guy. I haven't seen him a lot over the years, but he hasn't changed much. His body is still lean and muscular. He still cuts his hair the same way—military style.

I don't know how old he is, but I'm certain he's a lot older than he looks. The only thing that's really changed over the years is that his hair has turned grey. It looks good though; kind of majestic even. He definitely looks like the kind of guy who's been around and just knows stuff.

As I was studying him, I realized that in some ways his physique is kind of like mine—a much older version of course. He must have read my mind because he looked at me like he was sizing me up too.

"You've been working out... A lot by the looks of it," he said.

"Yup." I flexed a bicep to show off a little.

"You know, you remind me a little bit of myself when I was your age," he said with a nod of approval. "Of course you are your own man. You aren't me. You aren't your father either. You're just you. So... are you wondering why I chose the park for us to spend this special day together?"

"Sure."

"Because this is the perfect place for me to share some very important lessons with you today."

"Lessons? Lessons for what?" I asked.

"You'll see," he said. "But once you learn these lessons, you'll have a deeper understanding of how to make your way in this world. You'll be better prepared to grow into someone people will respect and look up to. You won't have to settle for anything either. You'll be able to choose work you love, but also work that has purpose and meaning. You'll be in a position to be a leader too. People will respect you as a leader, and as a leader, in one way or another, you'll be well compensated for your contributions to making this world a better place for yourself and everyone else you come in contact with."

"That sounds good," I said thoughtfully. A leader? I hadn't really thought of myself as a leader, but I liked the sound of it. I liked the thought of being able to make decisions instead of being told what to do.

Granddaddy continued, "The first of these very important lessons is represented by this walk in the park. The lesson is that the simple things in life really can be some of the best things in life. Always make time in your busy life to enjoy them. Take a relaxing walk in the park. Take time to appreciate a sunrise or a sunset. Take a moment to admire a bird in flight. Remember and cherish your first kiss with your girlfriend."

He stopped walking and looked straight at me. "Don't let your life get so complicated that you end up negotiating away your values and not living up to your highest potential. Never forget the miracle ***you*** truly are, or all the miracles you're surrounded by every day. When you take the time to look at the world and begin to see all the possibilities around you, you'll always be able to find the strength to do what's right." He smiled and then looked up at the sky.

"Yup. Definitely a storm on the way."

I looked up at the sky and then at him, but he'd started walking again. My gut was telling me there was some truth to what he was saying, but I didn't really see him often enough to know if I could trust everything he said. Maybe he was just a cool older guy who told good stories.

He had an aura of authority though, and talked with the deliberate wisdom of an old soldier. I knew he'd seen a lot as a World War II fighter pilot, but I wasn't convinced he could smell the "coming of rain". I sniffed the air, but I couldn't smell anything. I couldn't see any shelter to run to even if it did start to rain. He must have been reading my mind.

"It'll be okay. I've weathered many storms in my life much worse than the one headed our way," he said clapping a hand on my shoulder. "I know you're only 16 years old, but I have the feeling you might have already weathered a few storms worse than the one headed this way too."

At first, I thought he was talking about the rain, but Granddaddy had a way of talking about things that made a person think. It was one of the things I liked about him.

Granddaddy continued walking. "As a matter of fact, as unusual as it may sound, I love rain storms now. Maybe you will too someday. They remind me of the awesome power of my Creator. Rain doesn't discriminate. If we get caught in the rain, it will soak us without a care for who we are or where we came from. It doesn't matter how soaked we get either. The enduring power of the sun will indiscriminately dry all of us off.

"Getting caught in the rain reminds me of how strong and how weak we can be at the exact same time. The rain and the sun are two more of life's miracles working together to remind us of life's cycles. Sort of like the movie *The Lion King* and the circle of life it described. Of course the big difference between the real thing and the movie is that the movie is the same every time you watch it. The rain, the sun, our lives... well... they're all a little bit more unpredictable. When you pay attention though, it gets easier to figure out what's important and what's trivial. If things seem overwhelming, just look up at the sky and suddenly your problems will seem small alongside all the majesty and wonder going on up there."

I looked up at the sky again, trying to figure out what Granddaddy was saying without having to ask him to explain it. His words made me think about thunderstorms and maybe even about other kinds of storms I'd gone through over the years. I remember what they'd felt like and I didn't like thinking about those times anymore than I liked the thought of getting caught in the rain today. What did he know about me? Did he know about my past? How could he? He wasn't around enough to know that much, but he was right about one thing, I did have a tough life.

School wasn't easy for me. Home wasn't much better. It was always loud, chaotic, and stressful, just like it was for everyone else who lived in my neighborhood. At least I'd learned a few things to make it easier to deal with. And what could I do about it anyway? That was the way life was for us. And even though my life wasn't perfect, I still had a better life than a lot of other people. At least I had my sports and a great girlfriend.

My girlfriend is the best thing in my life. She's tall, very athletic, and beautiful. She has big beautiful brown eyes and long flowing hair that's brown with blond highlights. Sometimes she reminds me of one of those music divas—minus the attitude. She's awesome at basketball and track and is a great person with a heart of gold. She's perfect, except for the fact that she's always losing her keys.

I think it's so cute when she loses them. I try not to laugh while she fumbles through her purse trying to find them. After a few failed attempts, she gets frustrated, sighs, and then tips her purse upside down, spilling the contents onto the table. Then presto, like magic, the keys are there, sitting on top of the rubble she calls "all her stuff".

I know how fortunate I am to have someone like her in my life because most of my friends aren't as lucky. They don't have someone solid in their life; someone they can count on and hold on to when times are tough. It probably feels to them like the sun doesn't shine much in their world. For them, it's dark skies and storm clouds most of the time. My girlfriend is like the sun. I just feel better when she's around.

It's tough when you feel like there's no one around who cares. I guess that might be one of the reasons so many of my old friends have turned away from school, sports, and even the law. They don't feel like there's anybody who really cares about them. Instead, they turn to gangs and end up a part of all the drugs, crime, and fighting that comes along with them.

It doesn't seem that long ago that we used to laugh and play in the streets and didn't have to worry about looking over our shoulder all the time. We played sports and pretended we were superstars hitting home runs, scoring touchdowns, or sinking the winning basket.

I miss those days sometimes. We used to have such a great time. We had our sports and our friendships, but time kept moving and we started getting caught up in what was going on around us. Before too long, we were fighting in the streets too. After a while, we turned to different things.

I stuck with sports and joined teams. I learned it took discipline to get better and I liked it. I liked the routine. I learned about persistence, but my old friends didn't see the value of organized sports. To them, it looked like too much work and too much being bossed around. For me, it was an outlet. I got to channel the same frustration, anger, and aggression we all felt into something a whole other group of people cheered for.

I like how physically demanding the sports I play are. I

get a kick out of the fact that it's legal to hit the enemy as hard as I can on the football field without worrying about being arrested for it. I find it amazing that people praise me and admire me for brawling on the wrestling mat in front of stands full of bystanders instead of suspending me. Even the principal watches and then congratulates me after I've skillfully nailed my opponent to the ground.

With sports, I get to focus all my intensity into becoming a force to be reckoned with in both wrestling and football. Turning to sports made it easier for me to walk away from fighting in the streets.

Now I put my energy to good use by putting up a good fight in competitive sports. I know I'm only 16 years old, but I'm pretty lucky to have already figured out other ways to channel my anger. I use it to punish the weights in the weight room with a ferocity rarely seen in guys my age. I've grown muscle and developed incredible strength for my age too. Being so strong has also enabled me to keep up with the older varsity guys in both football and wrestling.

I know playing sports has helped keep me out of trouble with the police too. In my neighborhood, probably a lot of neighborhoods, you don't always have to be committing a crime to get the police to pay attention to you. They still might look at me now, but it's different.

Playing sports has created this weird phenomenon in my life. In general, people look at me differently. They don't look at me like I'm a thug or another "reject" from the streets. They don't talk about me as just another one of those kids that grew up in a "dysfunctional" family. Instead, people respect me.

Strangers say hi to me everywhere I go. They tell me they saw me play or wrestle or that they'd read about what I did in the newspaper. People are always congratulating me now. Once a kid even asked me for my autograph! It blows my mind that I get all this positive attention for putting up a good fight in sports rather than on the streets! Sometimes it's a little strange too because it feels like people are watching me and waiting to see what I'll do next. But maybe that's what people do anyway. They just kind of watch each other to see who's going to do something worth watching.

How strange life is! Sometimes my thoughts wander and I start thinking really deep about the things going on around me, or about things I read in school and then it's like I become the watcher. Sometimes I get really deep into my thoughts and start making weird paradoxical connections, like seeing the adults at school telling kids not to be angry and not to fight, but then turning around and praising me for putting up a good fight in sports.

I also think that in a bizarre way, my experience from the streets, and the anger I felt as a result of some of the things I've had to deal with have been beneficial to me. Would I have made the varsity wrestling team as a freshman without any formal training if I hadn't started on the streets?

I don't know. I know there's a big difference between a 14-year-old and an 18-year-old. 14 year olds are usually significantly over-matched and can't compete against 18 year olds. 14 year olds with no formal training just don't make varsity teams. But I did! Some people say I'm a natural, and maybe they're right, but I want to believe there's more to it than that. I mean… I'm the one who did it, right?

Okay, I might have gotten a head start with wrestling from fighting when I was younger. But then I learned about gladiators and I wondered if maybe they grew up dealing with some of the same stuff. Did Roman adults go around telling Rome's gladiators not to be angry or fight in the streets when they were growing up? Some of those ancient gladiators made it all the way to the Roman Coliseum!

I know we need order in this world, but I think it's a little bit ironic. When we're kids, they tell us not to fight, but we have famous warriors in our history books and famous prize fighters on TV. They tell us not to do it, but the better we are at it, the more handsomely paid and praised we are for it.

Sometimes it feels like there's a lot of distance between the streets and the arena. There wasn't really any "glory of the battle" when I was fighting—just survival. I didn't want to continue with the chaos of that path even though a lot of my old friends are still there. My decision to focus on sports has been much more productive than fighting in the streets and it keeps me out of trouble. I just wish my old friends had chosen sports over the streets too!

2

The Storm

"By the time a man realizes that maybe his father was right, he usually has a son who thinks he's wrong."

- Charles Wadsworth

I thought I felt a drop of rain splat on the rim of my ball cap and stuck my hand out, palm up to see if it was starting to rain. It wasn't. I was glad because I was feeling pretty fortunate to be spending time with my Granddaddy today. It's November 30th and it's my birthday. It's the greatest day for a birthday as far as I'm concerned because it lands right between the end of the fall sports season and the beginning of the winter sports season—perfect timing.

To tell the truth, I'm surprised he came around today. I haven't seen him in a long time and he didn't come by for my birthday last year. When my mom told me he was coming by today and wanted to talk to me, I was a little nervous. I thought maybe he was going to tell me he was dying or something crazy like that, but I heard him say to my mom, "Don't you worry about me. I've got way too many things to do and dyin' isn't on the list."

I guess we have that in common too. Like him, I have a very busy life. There's school, sports, and my morning paper route. I also have my part-time job at the gas station. I work there after practice on school nights and then the entire day on Sunday. Saturday is always game day, so I'm busy pretty much every minute of every day.

Some days I wish I had a few more hours to work with so it would be easier to get things done—like homework. There are definitely times when I end up winging it or not doing it at all. I know that's not good, but I seem to get by and somehow manage to pass my classes. In the end, I guess that's all that really matters, right?

Granddaddy hasn't said much yet, but he's already got me thinking. I don't think he wants to talk to me because he's dying either. He looks healthy. I think he wants to talk to me because he has something he wants me to hear. Weird, but he's a cool guy and I want to hear what he has to say.

Today's the perfect day because it's between seasons so I don't have practice or a game, and I don't have to be at work until much later. I wonder if he knew that before today. It would be nice if he had. It would mean he really did make the trip just to talk to me. I know he didn't spend much time with Pops when Pops was a kid, but I don't feel sorry for Pops because he did the same thing to me. He could have been different with me and spent time with me, but he didn't.

Maybe it runs in the family. Pops spends the same amount of time with me that his dad spent with him. I'm too busy to spend a lot of time with anyone, except for my girlfriend, and I'm not around for her as much as she would like either. Still, it got me thinking. If I have a son, will I end up doing the same thing to him?

From generation to generation, it looks like the cycle keeps repeating itself in my family. I wonder if it happened to Granddaddy too. It makes me think about my old friends. I don't know if I remember their dads being around much either. What if this doesn't just happen to people like me, or people in my neighborhood? What if it's happening to most people? What if it's the way it is in our society, and families aren't spending time together like they used to? Man, I'm just a regular philosopher today.

Isn't it weird how life works out sometimes though; how the same things cycle around in different kinds of ways? The pattern continues with just enough variation to make it harder to see. Most of us never even notice it because we're stuck right in the middle of it. We're too busy thinking about how everything is affecting us, all wrapped and trapped inside an invisible cycle. Is that what Granddaddy meant when he was talking about the cycle of life and the coming storm?

I don't know what happened between Granddaddy and Pops. All I know is that Granddaddy doesn't come around. Pops is an angry guy in general, but he does seem to get a certain kind of angry when Granddaddy shows up.

My mom says Granddaddy was never around when Pops needed him. Instead he was always too busy trying to make money and succeed. Every time Granddaddy comes around she tells me not to be like him. She says he neglected his kids in order to spend more time at the office, and that's why Pops is always angry. If Granddaddy had been there for him, then maybe Pops would have been more of a success and he wouldn't have any reason to drink.

I don't know though. Pops hasn't been around for me and I succeed once in a while. Maybe not all the time, but when I do, it's because I did something pretty good. Truth is, I don't much care what Pops thinks about what I do. Well, maybe that's not exactly true, I do care, I just don't let caring stop me from doing.

After I'd won my first wrestling match, I was so excited. As soon as I got home, I told Pops. No response. So I went to my bedroom and closed the door. I felt so stupid. Why did I think anything I did would impress him? My mom came into my room and told me that success comes from inside. That it's something you feel when you look at the results of your contribution. It doesn't come from other people, titles, or your reputation. You can have all those things without feeling like you've succeeded.

It made me feel a little better, but it also made me wonder if Pops thought of himself as a success. Probably not. If what mom says is right about Pop's and Granddaddy's relationship, then it sounds like Pops is still rebelling against his father, and using that as his excuse to drink too much and treat his family badly.

Mom says that a lot of people have the formula for success wrong. They chase the outer world rather than their inner world. What they need to do is to take the time to understand what Jesus was really saying when he told us the Kingdom of Heaven was within each of us. God bless mom! She really is the rock and bread of this family!

But how crazy is it that after all this time Pops is still

using Granddaddy as his excuse? Are adults really just big kids running around with the same emotions and feelings as kids my age? I might only be 16, but it seems to me that Pops is the pot calling the kettle black. If he was so upset by the way Granddaddy treated him, then why doesn't he make an effort to spend time with me?

I guess the big difference with the cycle this time around is that I'm fine with him not being around much. When he does come home, it's usually late and he's usually drunk. He's angry, mean, and abusive. He doesn't do it now, not since my big brother put a stop to it, but he used to come home and start beating on all of us... me, my brother, and my mother. I've never been able to figure out what we did to make him so angry. I've thought about it a lot though.

The thing is, none of us had anything to do with the fact that Granddaddy wasn't there for him. None of us even existed when that happened. Maybe when he looks at me all he sees is the underachiever he is, and it's too painful for him. Maybe he hates me because I actually succeed at stuff and he hates that I can do things he didn't, or couldn't do. Is it possible he's jealous and was trying to beat the success right out of me? To tell you the truth, I don't know what he sees when he looks at me.

Pops wasn't home today when Granddaddy arrived and I'm glad he wasn't. I've never talked with Granddaddy about Pops and I don't want to. I'm just glad to spend time with him. It's nice to have someone talking to me instead of yelling at me. I like telling him about the things I've done. He nods like he knows what I'm talking about. Maybe I'm an overachiever like he is. I'd like to think I'm more like Granddaddy than Pops. I definitely have a burning desire not to be anything like Pops.

It makes me angry to think about this, but if Pops had been a real dad instead of an angry frustrated man pretending to be my father, I believe my life would be better. At the very least, my stomach probably wouldn't freeze up every time I hear him come home at night wondering what kind of mood he's in. If he'd cared about me, he could have taught me what it means to be a good dad. Instead, he taught me how to be angry. I still get angry, but I know the difference between taking it out on a person and using it as fuel for a workout.

When I'm a dad I'm going to do a better job. I don't exactly know how to do it—it's not like Pops showed me what a good dad does. But I know I won't treat my kids the way Pops treats me. I'm going to be there for my kids. I will break this cycle! I will be the one who everyone in this future family tree looks up to as the one who changed it all, the hero!

I looked sideways at Granddaddy and could just barely hear him humming. I don't know if he was humming an actual song, but to me it was more evidence that he's nothing like Pops. I've never seen him angry and never heard him yell—not even at Pops. It makes me wonder if he ever gets angry.

If Granddaddy had been the kind of dad who hit, I think I'd know. I'm not the only guy with a dad who hits. I know a lot of guys who've been hit by their dads. It's not like they announce it, we all just kind of know. I guess that means their dads are angry too. Is that the reason so many of my old friends seem to be getting angrier as time goes by? Or is that the way it is in rough and tough neighborhoods and schools like mine?

I don't want to believe all this anger is normal, but it seems to be normal where I live. People are always yelling about something in my neighborhood. When I go to a friend's home there's usually someone yelling there too. My teachers and coaches are constantly yelling at the students and athletes. All I see around me is a very loud world full of chaos. I think it's normal because I'm used to it. I sure hope it isn't like this everywhere on the planet. It would suck to find out the whole world is like this.

But Granddaddy's not angry, and I know he grew up somewhere around here. I wonder where he lives now. Maybe he lives in another part of the world the rest of us don't know about. If he does live in some special place, who else lives there and what kinds of things do they talk about? Can I go there or is it so secret it's closed off to people like me because of where we come from? What's the weather like there? Is it always sunny or do they have storms like the one Granddaddy can smell coming?

If there is a place like that, I hope Granddaddy tells me about it. Maybe he's trying to figure out if I'm good enough to move there. I want to be, but I don't know if I am. Or maybe this other place is some kind of crazy secret society or cult!

I don't know if there is such a place; there probably isn't. It's just that philosopher part of me getting carried away and thinking all these crazy thoughts. What I can't figure out is if Granddaddy really did grow up in the same crazy, loud, chaotic world I'm living in. According to my mom, he did. If he did, then how did he escape?

I know he fought Hitler in World War II. Maybe he learned something from that, but he doesn't talk about it and I don't ask. If he was around more I might, but he isn't. Instead, I listen to him hoping he'll tell me more stories about his life.

There are a lot of things I like about him. He's always so peaceful for one. It's like he likes himself and because he does, it makes it easy for people to like him right back.

He's confident too. He doesn't act like he knows everything, he acts like he's happy knowing what he knows. He always seems to have someplace to go, but he's not nervous about getting there either. When he's ready to leave, he just looks at his watch and says "Would you look at the time. Gotta hit the road."

3

Skate to Where the Puck is Going!

"Efforts and courage are not enough without purpose and direction."

- John F. Kennedy

"Let's go this way," Granddaddy said pointing to the right. "If I remember correctly, there's a pavilion with a red picnic table on the other side of those big pine trees."

I thought I knew this park by heart, but I couldn't remember ever seeing a pavilion with a picnic table.

"We can sit and let the pavilion shelter us from the storm."

"Can you really smell the rain coming?" I asked.

"I sure can," he replied with a big smile and then sniffed at the air. "It's even stronger now. It's going to start raining any time now."

I gave him a sideways look.

"Don't look so doubtful. Being able to smell a storm brewing is an easy skill to develop. All you have to do is start paying attention to what the air smells like. Take a deep breath when you go outside. After a while you'll be able to tell when it's going to rain or snow or be sunny just by the smell of the air. Can you do that?"

I nodded my head and took a deep breath. I still couldn't smell anything, but I was willing to give it a try.

Granddaddy smiled. "Good. Glad we got that out of the way because I have a lot more secrets I want to share with you today."

He was going to share secrets with me? Secrets? Actual secrets? My heart quickened.

"Well, a lot of people think of them as secrets simply because they've never heard them before. When we started walking, I didn't use the word secrets though, I used the word lessons. I used that word first because I wanted to see if you'd be interested in hearing what I had to say."

"I'm in. I want to hear whatever you have to say. Did you think I wouldn't listen because you used the word lesson?"

Granddaddy shrugged. "Not exactly... I just know from experience that sometimes people are willing to hear what you have to say and sometimes they aren't. We all know what lessons are. Sometimes we learn them in school. Other times we learn them as a result of something we did. Did you ever burn your finger on a match?"

"Probably."

"Have you done it again?"

"That wouldn't be very smart...doing it twice."

"You're right. You learned your lesson the first time. The way I figure it, a lesson is something you can learn, but after you have a real life experience with applying a lesson, it turns into something more. I could sit here and recite the lessons I'd like you to learn, but that's not what I have in mind. The secrets I want to share with you can be used to build a meaningful and successful life. For example, do you know what the great hockey player Wayne Gretzky said when he was asked what the secret to his success was?"

"No." I answered.

He leaned closer and said "He said he never skated to where the puck was, but rather to where the puck was going to be. He always planned ahead and that's what made him a success and a superstar."

"Hmm, I guess that makes sense," I replied.

"It does," Granddaddy said. "You must always plan ahead. It's a way of preparing for whatever happens next. Like right now. I planned ahead and now when it starts raining we'll be dry instead of getting soaked."

"So coming here was part of a plan," I said.

"Well, I knew it was going to rain, and I knew I wanted to talk to you somewhere where there wouldn't be a lot of other people around. I remembered this place, so yes, I planned ahead."

I nodded and tried not to smile. How cool was it that he had taken the time just to talk to me.

"But there's another important thing about this plan I want you to be aware of. I didn't just plan to keep myself dry. I planned it so we would both be dry."

It was starting to rain now and Granddaddy nodded his head thoughtfully. "The other thing that made Gretzky great was that his planning didn't create a level of success that only benefited him. His plan, and ultimately his success, had a huge impact on the whole team's success.

"When you make plans, you want to remember that a lot of the time your success has the power to influence the success of the people around you whether it's as part of a team, at home, or out in your community. So when you decide which dreams you want to pursue and start planning for, make sure your vision includes success for the people around you too. It doesn't matter whether we're talking about sports or life either. Most people are too mentally lazy to think about anything beyond getting what they want, so they don't put any extra energy or thought into planning for anyone or anything beyond themselves. Instead, they nonchalantly wing it hoping no one will notice, or that someone else will be there to pick up their slack. And then they brag about winging it like it's something to be proud of!"

Granddaddy shook his head. "You're already a good planner and you're only 16. That's good because as you get older you're going to see a lot of people who are still winging it.... It's one thing to wing it when you haven't studied as hard as you should have for a test. It's another thing to wing it when you have a family that's relying on you."

I wondered if Granddaddy somehow knew I hadn't studied for my last test. I had definitely winged it. Still... I got a C+.

"When people don't take the time to make plans, they give up any control they might have over the results they're going to get. They have almost no chance of winning. Worse than that, they aren't likely to be in a position to help others. Do you know what a kayak looks like?"

Granddaddy was talking like I think sometimes, moving from one thought to another without a pause in between, but I was determined to keep up with him. "Sure. I know what a kayak is."

"It's like they've gotten into a kayak and started floating down a lazy river. It might be okay for a while, but as soon as it starts getting rough, or they want to stop or change direction, they can't because they didn't plan well enough to bring a paddle. Without a paddle, they're at the mercy of the river currents. They might even start picking up speed or hit white water rapids. They might be heading towards a damn or waterfall. Will they survive? Maybe, but if they'd planned on bringing a paddle, they would have been a lot better prepared and might have even enjoyed the challenges the river presented."

"You'd have to be pretty dumb to forget a paddle," I said.

"Well, what if they didn't know they needed a paddle?" Granddaddy asked and shook his head. "I know that sounds weird, but we're not really talking about a kayak. We're talking about people setting out to do something figuring they'll be able to wing it. If no one tells them they need a paddle, and they don't put enough thought or planning into it before they step into the kayak, how are they going to know they need one?"

"That's crazy." I said.

"It is." He replied. "Eventually, these people realize the trouble they're in and either panic or shut down. Either way, they started out without the tools or knowledge they needed to keep themselves out of trouble. Even if they somehow manage to come through it okay, it's not like they can take credit for what they've done because they didn't do anything. They can't feel like they've accomplished or achieved anything either... because they haven't.

I stared at the rain drops starting to drip off the edge of the roof thinking about how stupid it would be to get into a kayak without a paddle. Then I turned and smiled at him. "I can honestly say that I don't think I've ever done anything that stupid."

He looked at me thoughtfully. "As far as I know, you haven't, but people don't plan to be dumb. They just end up doing dumb things when they don't plan. What if it was you in that kayak and it was a two-seater kayak and you had your five year old son in the front seat?"

I frowned. "I'd make sure I had a paddle and that he was wearing a life preserver."

"Exactly. But you're already a good planner. Too many people aren't, and when they aren't, it's the people who are counting on them that suffer the most. And I'm not going to lie to you. Some people wing it most of the time and do surprisingly well for a while. But that's an exception; not the rule. People who experience success without any planning or effort have no idea what to do when things stop going their way. They never had a plan A which means they don't have a plan B. Planning your life gives you options.

"Gretzky's plan A was to skate to where the puck was going to be. We have to do the same thing. Figure out where we want to be and then make a plan to get there. If we don't, trust me, society will be right there creating its own plan for you, and chances are it won't be a plan you're going to enjoy. A life handed to you by default is rarely a meaningful, successful, or fulfilling life."

I thought about my old friends and how they never talked about their plans for the future. Well, except for being a professional baseball, football, or basketball player. Was society creating a plan for them? "Well, I think I do plan ahead," I said. "I think about my future all the time. Is that what you mean?"

"Yes. That's exactly what I mean. How do make your plans?"

I wasn't sure I wanted to tell him. I hadn't really ever told anyone about my plans, but I took a deep breath and started talking. "Well, I have this thing called a Mission Statement."

Granddaddy nodded his approval. "How'd you know to do that?"

"I found this book by Anthony Robbins and read about it in there. I thought it sounded like a cool idea so I wrote one. Now when I get up in the morning I read it before I do anything else. I also read it at night. It's the last thing I do before I turn out the light. Anthony says that doing this will program my mind for success."

"Great! What's your statement about?"

I shrugged. "It's just a few simple sentences about my goals and about the kind of person I want to be."

"How'd you decide what to write?"

"The book said to visualize the future I wanted, so every morning for the last couple of years while I was walking my morning paper route, I'd imagine what it would be like doing some of the things I really wanted to do... like making the varsity teams in both football and wrestling.

And you know what? It's working! I've already made the varsity teams in both sports and I'm just a sophomore in high school!"

"And you know what?" Granddaddy said. "You're using the exact same strategy Gretzky used. He skated to where he knew the puck would be. The puck wasn't there when he started moving, but he planned it just right and the puck was there when he arrived. You're doing the same thing; turning the invisible into the visible by planning, and then expecting to see it. You're pretty smart for a teenager."

I couldn't believe I was having this conversation. People were always congratulating me and stuff, but I never talked about how good turning my dreams into reality felt. I didn't want to brag, but it didn't feel like bragging with Granddaddy.

"You know," he continued. "It's okay to feel good about what you've accomplished. You've done a good job. I've been very impressed with what you've achieved so far. I know you were the captain of your freshmen football team and you're the only sophomore on the varsity team right now."

I stared at him. How did he know that?

"Furthermore, I know that as a freshmen wrestler you lost your first wrestle-off to one of your team's returning varsity wrestlers. I know you broke the middle finger on your left hand during that wrestle-off, and that you refused to take the school bus home. Instead you walked the five miles. And when you thought nobody was watching, you cried out with the pain. If I know you as well as I think I might, it wasn't just because of the broken finger, it was because you lost your first wrestle-off."

"You saw that?" I asked feeling a little embarrassed.

"I did. I also know that even after the doctors told you you'd have to sit out most of the season, you kept learning, improving, and wrestling with that broken finger. If I'm remembering it right, it was only a few weeks later when you beat that same varsity wrestler in another wrestle-off. In fact, you continued beating him at every weekly wrestle-off. That's how you earned and kept earning your spot in the starting line-up on the varsity wrestling team as a freshman."

"How do you know all that?" I asked.

With his face visibly turning sad Granddaddy responded. "Even though you haven't seen me around much, that doesn't mean I haven't been around and paying close attention to what's going on in your life."

"I never knew," I said. I wasn't sure how I felt about it either. He had been there? He had seen me? It would have been so great to share my success with someone. "Why didn't you let me know? Why didn't you say something or let me know you were there?"

"Listen," Granddaddy started, his voice very serious, "Sometimes things are complicated and this is one of those times. At any rate, I'm here right now, so let's stay on track. You were telling me about how you visualized the invisible into the visible."

"Well, I visualized my goals so often, and they were so clear in my mind, I was able to break them down into small specific details and then fit them into a timeline. I had this past football season mapped out at least a year ahead of time. One of the things I visualized was our football team having a great season. Almost all of it turned out the way I had imagined too. We even made it to the playoffs. You're right... I made the invisible, visible!

"Yup. Good example."

"I've also been visualizing wrestling too. I'm expecting our wrestling team, and myself, to be very competitive and place in the state tournament this coming season. I can already see my junior year and I've developed a sense of certainty that both the football and wrestling teams will go even further in the playoffs next year. For my senior year, I'm visualizing both teams being unstoppable and winning the state championships. Finally, I'm certain I'm going to win the individual state wrestling title at 145 pounds."

"Wow," Granddaddy said raising his eyebrows. "The 145 pound weight class is a pretty tough weight class. Aren't you wrestling the 132 class this year?"

"Yup," I answered confidently.

"So, you're a sophomore in high school right now, and through this visualization you know how much you will weigh in two years when you're a senior?"

"Yup. In fact, I'm certain of it. Not only do I know how much I will weigh in two years, but I also know I'll be the captain of both the football and wrestling teams. And, I'll be the 145 pound state wrestling champ!" I suddenly realized that for the first time I was saying all of this out loud to someone. It was weird but it was also kind of easy because I really believed what I was saying.

I couldn't stop myself from talking. "I know it sounds like a lot, but I've been visualizing this for so long that it doesn't feel out of reach anymore. I expect to win and I do. I mean... don't get me wrong, I still get nervous before each wrestling match or football game, but it's different now. It feels like my destiny. All I have to do is follow my plans and the winning and success will continue. I know how it sounds, but what can I say. It's what I believe. It's what I know."

"The ancient Greeks called it "hubris. We call it cockiness," Granddaddy said with a big smile on his face. "But you're right. What you're talking about is different. Great people always start with absolute belief in their minds before they are great in the outside world. I like what I'm hearing and I can see you're really fired up about this. It's impressive. You're a teenager and you already know how to write and use a mission statement. You've already figured out how to take your planning to the next level using visualizations, and it sounds like you already know how to use your visualizations to add details to your planning. Most adults don't know anything about either of those two strategies. But you keep right on doing what you've been doing."

"So you don't think it's too cocky to think that way?"

"No, I don't," Granddaddy replied without hesitation. "Contrary to what a lot of people think, success is not hubris or cockiness. We should all strive to live our lives to the fullest. Our forefathers, the framers of our revered Constitution, understood this and made sure we'd all have the inalienable right to the pursuit of happiness. Being successful makes people feel happier and more fulfilled."

I thought about that.

"Look at it this way," he said. "If you don't make decisions about what you want to do or where you want to be in the future, then you're stuck back in that kayak without a paddle. So keep reading your mission statement. Put your emotions into it so you really feel it when you say those words. Keep visualizing and programming yourself for success. As long as you keep doing those things, I believe you'll not only fill the tall order you've written for yourself, but I also think you'll surprise yourself and achieve even more than you've ever dreamed!"

Granddaddy turned to face me. "The big trick for you right now is to carry that positive way of thinking, planning, and working over to the classroom. You've got to do better than those C's you've been getting."

My mouth opened, but nothing came out.

"Hey," Granddaddy said, "don't be so surprised. I told you... I've been paying attention. And now that we've been talking, I know you'll be able to figure out how to use a mission statement and visualizations to step up your class work too. By the time you master that, you'll be ready to start thinking and planning for your life way beyond school and sports. You're already having a positive effect on your teammates and your school with your success. Think of the impact you can make when you take all your skills out into the world."

"Wow!" I said. "That sounds really great... and kind of scary all at the same time."

"I think the word you're looking for is empowering," Granddaddy said.

"Yeah.... You're right," I said nodding my head. "It's empowering. It's a lot to think about, but I like it."

4

The Pain of Regret

"People think it's too hard to do the extra work that's needed to excel. But what's really hard is living with the regret of knowing you could have done more."

- Daniel Blanchard

We were quiet for a while, listening to the rain.

"Now, getting back to talking about planning," Granddaddy said. "It's a sad truth, but very few people plan their lives and that's one of the reasons there are so many people in this world living below their potential. I want to make sure you understand that people don't plan to fail in life on purpose. Most people just fail to plan. The trick is to not judge those people too quickly.

"Don't think people fail simply because they're unintelligent. There are brilliant people who never experience success and regular people who experience extraordinary success. The fact is, most people have never been told the secrets of how to succeed in life. No one helped them understand that they had options other than the ones they'd been surrounded with while they were growing up. That's one of the reasons I'm sharing these secrets with you today. I don't want you to end up like so many of your classmates will... living a life without direction or inspiration.

"I won't," I replied.

Granddaddy chuckled. "I know *you* won't. But when you see it happen to someone you know, you might be tempted to think it's their own fault for not trying hard enough. Sometimes it's because no one ever took the time to teach them how. The secrets I'm teaching you today aren't taught in school. Most parents don't know them because they weren't taught them at home or in school when they were growing up either.

"Today, kids are only getting a partial education at home, at school, and out in society. When your classmates grow up and become parents themselves, most of them still won't have heard any of these secrets. If they don't know them, then they won't be able to teach them to their kids either.

"It's a cycle that keeps playing out, generation after generation of potentially great and fully capable children getting only portions of the knowledge they need to live the life of their dreams. Doesn't mean they won't try, but most will give up at some point and then end up living well below their true potential. Have you ever heard of the 80/20 rule?"

"No," I answered.

"Well, I'll start explaining it using your school as an example. I could say that 80% of the student body is made up of good kids who don't really cause any problems while the other 20% always seem to be getting in trouble. As a result, your school might get a bad reputation depending on how bad the 20% is.

"It can work in the other direction too, like with grades. 20% of the students are getting the best grades. The kids in that higher 20% group are going beyond the call of duty and excelling at their class work. Think about what happens when they get out of school and get jobs. The 80/20 rule applies in the workplace too. There, the top 20% very often end up carrying the load for the 80% who've given up trying to get into the top 20%. Does that make sense?" Granddaddy quizzed.

"I think so. Now that I'm thinking about it, there are definitely athletes in my school who give everything they have. Maybe that's why they do better than the others." I replied.

"That's probably accurate." Granddaddy said. "What would you say if I told you 20% of the people in this world control about 80% of the money and resources?"

"Is that true?" I asked.

"It is. And it's not because the 20% is made up of people who know how to work the system, or because they inherited all their money. A majority of the people in that 20% have worked long and hard for their success. The idea that they haven't is a cop-out people outside the 20% fall back on when they don't know how to bring more money or success into their own lives. Instead, they look at everything those other people have and complain that life just isn't fair."

Granddaddy shook his head. "Furthermore, those kinds of ideas are disempowering. So don't ever give in to the temptation of going down that road. If something in your life isn't working right, don't blame other people or the system. As soon as you start putting energy into blaming someone else, you aren't putting energy into doing something about it. Take responsibility for your own life and ownership of your energy so you get to be the one who decides where it will do the most good."

"Okay," I said. "I get what you're saying… Don't blame other people, or say that something isn't fair."

Granddaddy nodded and was quiet for a minute. "The other thing about people claiming that life isn't fair is that they'll say it when they don't feel like there's anything they can do. For example, did you know that one out of every two marriages ends up in divorce?"

I shook my head.

"One of the biggest reasons people get divorced is because of money. When you first look at this problem, it's easy to look at the money issue and decide it's because one of them isn't working hard enough. But there are a lot of different ways money can play a role.

"Say the couple starts out okay, but then they have a baby and now they need more money than they have. Babies tend to cry a lot when they don't get their diapers changed. Diapers cost money though, so maybe the parents can't change the diapers as often as they should because they can't afford to. Their baby keeps crying because he or she wants a dry diaper. It's a tough situation and extremely stressful for the parents. Some parents just don't know how handle the stress and end up making terrible choices. All that stress is one of the reasons there are so many abused and neglected children in this world."

"Are diapers expensive?" I asked.

"Anything you need and don't have the money to buy becomes expensive in your mind. Money can become a huge stress producer for anyone though—not just parents. That stress can lead to all kinds of bad choices. Is there any such thing as a happy, generous, kind, well-adjusted criminal who isn't out to make money?" Granddaddy shook his head. "Money may not be the number one reason people do bad things, but I bet it's in the top three."

My mouth tightened. "I didn't realize money was one of the reasons parents abuse their kids. I've heard Mom and Pops fighting over money, but... I—"

"Hold on. That's not exactly what I said. The point I was trying to make is that when it comes to money, people don't always make good decisions. When they make bad decisions, the people around them usually end up suffering with the consequences too. Money is not the only reason people struggle with being good parents. I just used that as an example to help you understand that having enough money is a problem a lot of people struggle with.

"For some people, money is an issue that never goes away. They don't realize there are other things they can do. They don't know other choices and options exist because no one ever took the time to explain them. They only know what's in their pocket. Even if you told them, a lot of those people are so used to having empty pockets and storm clouds hanging around them that it would take more than an idea to get them motivated."

I looked out at the clouds. They were moving fast now. "You mean like those clouds out there?"

"In some ways, yes," he answered. "But if you notice, those same storm clouds are headed our way too."

As if on cue, the rain really started coming down.

"Everybody has storm clouds in their life," Granddaddy continued. "We've all experienced the unrelenting downpours that sometimes come along with them too. What I'm saying is that there are people who don't have the resources or know-how to protect themselves from the storms life sends their way. For them, those storms are a constant stress. One storm hits them and before they have a chance to recover from that one, another storm comes along."

The wind was picking up too. I moved a little closer to the center of the table to keep from getting wet.

"Those storms start invading their dreams and waking them up in the middle of the night. That kind of constant stress does something to people and they end up making even more bad choices. They might start putting on extra weight or become so grouchy or mean that they alienate their families and friends. They get angry and blame anything and everyone around them. Stress is a lot like a parasite. Once it takes hold, its roots dig deeper and deeper into a person's hopes and dreams."

"That's a pretty scary thought," I said.

"You're right. It is," Granddaddy agreed. "It's tough to handle life's storms when you don't feel like you have any options. Never-ending stress is one of the reasons many good and able people turn to overeating, smoking, alcohol, drugs, or even meaningless sex. Each one of those is a way of temporarily escaping the weight of all the storms and stress hanging over their heads. When people do these things they get to forget—at least for a little while—about the distance between who they are and who they might have been. Their vices are like temporary shelters against the constant onslaught of storms."

"I know some people who do drugs," I said. "They've tried to get me to do them too. They say it's fun."

"I don't doubt they say that. But let me ask you this. Are they people who have a plan?"

I thought about that for a minute. "I guess not, unless you consider figuring out how to get high without getting caught a plan."

"Well, maybe you're right. That is a plan, but what do they get at the end of it? Nothing worth having. All those activities... drugs, alcohol, smoking, overeating, and promiscuous sex have a way of sucking the life right out of you. Eventually, people who use those things as a way of escaping their storms look in the mirror and see a person they barely recognize. Because they never knew there was another way, they'll cave into the idea that they're just another victim of a world that doesn't care. They'll surrender to their circumstances and give up the idea that there's anything they can do to change what's happened. They accept that they are helpless."

I just stared at the floor.

"So here's the thing. I'm not telling you this to make you feel bad. I'm telling you this so you can grasp how amazing the stuff you're doing really is. When your friends tried to get you to take drugs you could have said yes. But you didn't. You have plans and you chose to follow them instead. There might not be a lot of physical distance between you and the people you know who are doing drugs right now—some of them are probably sitting right next to you in school—but where will they be in ten years. Where will you be in ten years if you keep following your plans?

"They'll be stuck in a kayak without a paddle heading for a waterfall?" I offered.

"Ah... you're paying attention," Granddaddy said with a smile on his face. "And when they are, they won't be in any position to help the others around them—not even their own children. So the 80/20 rule continues to exist because it gets passed on from one generation to the next. Dad doesn't know what a paddle is so he can't teach his son what a paddle is either.

"The sad thing is that everybody has the power to do something. Everybody. Most of the 80% has just stopped trying. They believe other people have all the power while they have none. In other words, they have become both helpless and hopeless. But it's easy to understand. None of their parents, friends, school guidance counselors, or college advisors knew there was anything to share beyond academia. Sadly, the conversation you and I are having is rare."

"Wow. Listen to you! You're all fired up today Granddaddy!" The words had charged out of my mouth before I had a chance to think about how they might have sounded. "I'm sorry. I didn't mean to throw all that attitude your way. It's just that I can tell you feel very strongly about what you're saying... and I'm glad to be here and all... but why today? Why are you so fired up and insisting that I have to learn these secrets today? I mean...."

"Well, today is your birthday. And I know you don't know this, but 60 years ago today, was also my 16th birthday. We have the same birthday!" Granddaddy announced proudly. "60 years ago today, I ran away from my hot-tempered, overbearing father. I lied about my age and joined the army-air force to fight against Hitler. Shortly after I enlisted, I met Colonel Reynolds of the 475th group and my whole life changed. November 30th, 1941 was the most important day of my life. I chose to come here today to share with you what Colonel Reynolds shared with me."

"So today's your birthday too?"

"Yup. I kind of figured you didn't know."

"No... I didn't. Pretty cool though. Happy Birthday Granddaddy."

"Same to you," he said with a smile. "So that's why it had to be today. This day is very important to me, and hopefully it will be a day you'll never forget either. Colonel Reynolds shared these secrets with me on a day very much like this and now I get to pay it forward by sharing those secrets with you. My goal is that you'll always remember this day as the day someone took the time to share the secrets of life with you. This is a day that could change everything for you. By the time we're done, you might even look forward to the day when you get to pay it forward to someone else too."

My mind was racing and I could feel my heart beating. This felt right. I could just tell it was meant to happen. I wanted to say something but I didn't know what to say. Besides, I didn't want him to stop talking. I wanted to hear the secrets.

"Sixty-years ago today, I grabbed onto an opportunity

and landed in the midst of some incredible men. These were men who had been tough enough to get through the Great Depression, win a two-front war against overwhelming odds, and later to be called the Greatest Generation. I had the privilege of fighting alongside them under a couple of distinguished leaders named Colonel Reynolds and General Eisenhower. Together, we fought against another powerful and capable leader, Hitler."

"I learned about Hitler."

"I'm sure you did, but books don't do a good job of explaining what he used his leadership to do. His leadership almost destroyed the world. Hitler viciously killed 6 million Jews. He was literally trying to exterminate an entire race of people. It was a terrible time and even though I learned so many incredibly powerful secrets going through it, it took me a very long time to really understand them all.

"I tried to share some of them with my son... you know... your dad, but by the time I was able to figure out how to start explaining them, he was already past the point of being willing to listen to anything I had to say. It was a hard truth for me to accept, but there it was. I was too late to be the father and mentor he'd so desperately needed."

"What happened between you and Pops?" I quietly asked.

"That's complicated," Granddaddy answered. "I wasn't around much for him, and I know I haven't been around for you either, but there are reasons. And I know your dad has probably said some unpleasant things about me, but I'm here to tell you in person, I do have your best interest at heart. You're already headed in a good direction, but I don't have much time to share these secrets with you, and I do want to make sure you get the same life changing information I got without having to go fight in a war to get it."

"What do you mean you don't have much time?" I protested. "You said this was our special day and I thought we were spending the whole afternoon together. Where do you have to go?"

"That's not what I meant," Granddaddy said. "I promise, I'm not running out on you today. I'm here to spend as much time with you as *you* have available before *you* have to go to work. Wrestling season starts tomorrow, right?"

I nodded.

"Well, that means today is the only free day you're going to have for quite a while. That's what I meant when I said I don't have much time."

"Oh," I said and took a deep breath. "Hey, how'd you know wrestling starts tomorrow?"

"I told you, I've been paying attention."

I looked down at my sneakers. We were about as far inside the pavilion as we could get, but we were still getting hit by the rain blowing in. "Boy, this pavilion sure is beat up. I hope the roof stays on."

5

It's Already in YOU!

"What lies behind you and what lies in front of you, pales in comparison to what lies inside of you."

- Ralph Waldo Emerson

Granddaddy looked down at his shoes. They were getting wet too, but he didn't seem to mind. "I think it'll hold. And yes, it might be old and beat up like this picnic table, but we're okay while we're in here. We don't always need as much as we think we do. As a matter of fact, wanting more is where most of our unhappiness comes from. Have you ever heard of Buddha?

"No." I replied.

"He introduced a simple concept that's been around for thousands of years, but most people don't seem to grasp who Buddha was, or what his message was really about. Buddha taught people that the root of all unhappiness comes from wanting more and not being happy with what you have. He taught his followers that the true path to enlightenment is finding happiness with what you have. It isn't found at the end of a pursuit for what you don't have... but don't confuse what he said with complacency. We all still need to strive to do our best in life because when we do, we don't just improve the quality of our life, we also improve the quality of the lives of the people around us. If our efforts are based solely on gaining material possessions, we won't get the same results. For example, you've probably heard that I'm successful."

"I've heard some things," I said with a smile.

Granddaddy chuckled. "I bet you have. But what kind of car do I drive? I drive a regular every day, ordinary car. I could easily afford a big expensive car, but I chose to drive an average car and live in an average house."

"I always wondered about that," I said. "If you really are as successful as Pops complained you are, then why don't you live in a big fancy house and drive a big fancy car like other successful people?"

"That's a good question and I have an answer, but I'd like to tell you more about how this all started for me first. Basically, I'm asking you to trust me the same way I trusted Colonel Reynolds when I met him on my 16th birthday," said Granddaddy.

"Sure." I said nodding my head.

"Colonel Reynolds was a real man and a real leader. He was the kind of high quality person who only comes around once in a great while. His father was present at the 1914 Christmas Miracle of World War I and personally witnessed what destructive leadership was capable of doing. On Christmas day, the German and English soldiers stopped fighting and celebrated Christmas together in the middle of the battlefield in a space called "No Man's Land".

During their celebration, the enemies became friends and brothers and promised not to fight each other anymore. Unfortunately, their own officers had different plans. When their men refused to fight, they came down to the battlefield and forced the soldiers, at gunpoint, to break their promises and start killing each other again."

"That really stinks."

"You got that right. That Christmas Miracle could have ended World War I and possibly avoided World War II. It could have saved so many lives and put a stop to the immeasurable amount of misery and destruction war causes. It was a lesson in bad leadership that Colonel Reynolds' father never forgot. He in turn made sure his son learned it so he would always be able to tell the difference between good leadership and bad leadership.

"Great leaders like Colonel Reynolds get pushed to the front when they are needed the most—like during the war against Hitler. I was very grateful to have served under his leadership. He was an incredible man and the first person who ever took the time to tell me that if I wanted to be happy, then I should always strive to better myself. He'd say 'Shoot for the stars and miss with the moon." At first I didn't know what he meant. I'd heard the saying *Shoot for the moon. If you miss, at least you'll be among the stars*, but I'd never heard it the way he'd said it."

"That's the way I've heard it said too. Shoot for the moon," I said. "That's what I'm doing—shooting for the moon. Is that wrong?"

Granddaddy looked surprised. "Not at all. As long as you have a goal and you're taking steps to achieve your goal, you're going in the right direction. What Colonel

Reynolds explained to me was that we get to pick our goals. I know it sounds easy, but too many times the goals we pick have all kinds of limits on them. Think about your own goals, the ones you told me about. I can tell you're very determined, but do the goals you've set reflect everything you've ever dreamt about? If you could dream bigger, what would you dream?"

I hesitated and then whispered my answer. "The Olympics."

Granddaddy nudged my shoulder. "Now that's the kind of dream Colonel Reynolds would be impressed with. I'm impressed with it too. I'm also willing to bet that as you make your plans and work on achieving the goals you have right now, each one you accomplish moves you one step closer to being willing to consider the Olympics as an achievable goal rather than a pipe dream. Is that true?"

"Yeah, I guess so. I haven't really said it out loud to anyone before. It feels kind of weird."

"I can understand that. But here's what I want you to understand. You always want to have big dreams—dreams that are much further away than the moon. Our achievements are proof to our own selves of what we are capable of accomplishing. Our dreams give us a reason to continue reaching and striving beyond the goal we've just accomplished."

I nodded my head thoughtfully.

"When you reach for the stars, you'll have something to shoot for after you hit the moon. Another thing Colonel Reynolds said was, "Pursue the abilities of the elite with unwavering determination". He said that one a lot."

I chuckled. "That sounds like something my girlfriend

would say. She's always telling me to *dare to dream* and that I could probably be better at a lot of things—like studying. She says I get too zoned in on some things and because of that, I don't put enough effort into others.... That's also about the same time she puts her homework away so I can't see it. I don't think it's such a big deal. I get my homework done... most of the time."

"It sounds to me like you have a pretty special girlfriend," Granddaddy said smiling.

"She's great. But she's a girl too, so you know what that means... complicated." I looked at Granddaddy hopefully. "Is that one of the secrets you're going to tell me today? How to deal with complicated women?"

Granddaddy smiled and shook his head. "No... we have enough to talk about without going there. But it's nice to know she cares enough about you to give you some grief when you're looking for shortcuts instead of doing the work."

"I don't take shortcuts. I work hard."

"I don't think that's what she was saying and it isn't what I'm saying. But sometimes, settling for less is a shortcut. For example, if your grades aren't where you'd like them to be, the difference between a B+ and a C- is a kind of shortcut. It takes less work to get a C-. Letting someone else do the work for you, well, that's a shortcut too. What would happen if you took a shortcut when you were lifting by cutting your reps in half so you'd have more time outside of the gym? What would happen? How far would the results of that kind of workout strategy take you?"

I grimaced. "Not very far."

"Think of how it would affect your ability to achieve your goals."

"It would make them impossible."

"Well, I don't know about impossible, but I agree with you in that it would make them almost impossible. So can you see that when you put your effort into things, you can accomplish a lot more?"

"Yeah... I can see how that works."

"Okay, if you want to develop a habit of success, then get in the habit of putting your full effort into the things you want to accomplish, even if you don't think it's that important at first. Everything you accomplish is a result of your effort. If you want better results, then make sure you're giving yourself a better chance to succeed by putting in the work. Be pleased with your accomplishment when you hit the moon, but don't stop there. There's only one moon. There are lots of stars."

"Wow. That's a cool thought," I said.

"So is being an Olympian," Granddaddy said. "Have you thought about what your life will be like when you get there?" Granddaddy asked.

"I don't know. Maybe a little. I know it's going to take a lot of work to get there, but it'd be cool to have a nice car... I guess."

"Yup... Cars are great," he said. "They can definitely take you places."

I thought about Granddaddy's car. It wasn't all that fancy. "So how come you don't drive a fancy car? I mean... I don't know... Maybe it's none of my business."

"No, it's okay to ask, but I'm going to answer the real question you were trying to ask. Yes, I could afford to drive any car I want. I did a long time ago, but if I had followed Colonel Reynolds advice, I wouldn't have made that mistake."

"He said buying an expensive car is a mistake?"

"No he didn't say that, but that's what I heard. What he said was to strive for greatness, but live an average man's life." Granddaddy shook his head. "Believe me, I know how it sounds. I didn't get it at first either. It seemed to me that if I was making the money to afford it, then what was the harm in spending it? I found out what he meant the hard way.

"I bought that fancy car and it was something to see. When I drove it off the lot I couldn't wait to drive down my street and have everybody see me driving that car. I was proud of it... proud of the fact that I could afford it. But after I drove down my street the first time, that was it. My neighbors and friends saw it, agreed it was a nice car, and that was it. No one talked about it after that."

"I don't get it. What's wrong with that?"

"There was nothing wrong with their reaction. It was my reaction that was the problem. I didn't want them to talk about how nice the car was. I wanted them to realize I could afford to buy it. I was finally making good money and that car was evidence of it. No one cared though. In fact, it had the opposite effect. One of my neighbors even joked about me always buying stuff to show off. And then I understood what Colonel Reynolds was talking about. It's not how much money you have that matters, it's what you do with it.

"People spend their money to prove they are richer than their neighbor. They hoard their money so they can have more money than their neighbor. They hide their money because they're afraid their neighbor might try to steal it. The whole time they are doing those things, they aren't spending any time on being a good neighbor."

I smiled because I thought I understood the good neighbor part. It sounded a lot like what it was like to be on a team.

"As soon as I realized that," Granddaddy continued, "I stopped spending my money on things I didn't need and worked on being a better neighbor instead. Doing that didn't just make me a better person. It helped make me a wealthy person too."

"I think I know what you're talking about. That's what being on a team is like. You don't go around bragging about how good you are. If you do, your teammates aren't going to like it. But even when you don't brag, there are still going to be guys who look at you and think you're just lucky. During one football game I remember someone saying 'lucky catch' to me and it made me mad. I made that catch. Luck didn't have anything to do with it."

"It's good you know the difference. What some people call luck is actually when preparation meets opportunity. Most people think I'm very lucky. They think everything wonderful just drops into my lap, but there's a lot more to what they're thinking than that.

"People who don't know how to make things happen in their own life will often look at people who *are* making things happen and decide it's the result of luck. If they followed those successful people around though, they'd see all the work it takes to be successful. But, for whatever reason, a lot of people aren't interested in doing the same amount of work. They'd rather believe someone else's success is the result of luck so they can still have a glimmer of hope for succeeding without doing any of the work."

I chuckled. "I had a senior once ask me how I got so jacked and I told him about my workouts. I even offered to show him, but he wasn't interested. I think he was trying to figure out what my weaknesses were anyway. I was kind of his competition."

Granddaddy nodded. "Yup, some people are like that. They don't want to do the work. But think about what happens to them. If they don't do the work, the only glimmer of hope they have to cling to *is* luck. Good preparation puts people in a position to be ready when opportunity knocks. Then, when opportunity does knock, they're able to do things... like making an amazing catch.

"Do you know which catch I'm talking about?" I asked.

"I'm pretty sure. You've made a lot of great moves on the football field, but the one you're talking about was in the semifinal. What I want to make sure you realize is that the reason you were able to make that catch was because you put yourself in a position to make it. Luck didn't have anything to do with it! It was your preparation coming face-to-face with a real opportunity that you grabbed hold of. How many times have you done extra running and weightlifting outside of football or wrestling practice?"

"A bunch," I moaned.

Granddaddy continued. "And when you made the varsity teams, I'm sure there were plenty of people who thought you made it onto those teams because you were lucky rather than because you are a focused, determined, and committed athlete. I bet there were people who thought you were lucky when you battled your way to placing in the state wrestling tournament at the varsity level when you were just a freshman too. You know different. You know how much work you do, and you know why you do it—so you'll be ready when opportunity knocks. But can you see the danger in believing that luck is part of why people succeed?"

I shrugged because I wasn't exactly sure what I believed about luck.

"The danger with believing in luck is that it can make you feel hopeless and helpless all at the same time. Anytime you look at something you or somebody else has accomplished and you take skill or effort out of the equation, you'll struggle with figuring out how to make it happen again. Think about the catch you made. If you really believed it when you heard the words "lucky catch", what are the chances of you being able to make that catch again?"

"I'm not sure," I admitted.

"That's a good answer, and the reason you're not sure is because you used your skills to make that pivotal catch. If I take your skill and preparation out of the equation, I take away your confidence in your ability to do it again.

"People who believe they need luck to succeed, or decide that other people succeeded because they were lucky, are both helpless and hopeless. You can't prepare for luck. All you can do is sit and wait for it to strike. Even then, there's no guarantee it's going to come your way. People pray for luck when they don't have faith in their ability to make things happen. Does that make sense?"

"Yeah, it's like Gretzky... he wasn't lucky, he was

prepared and ready to move to where the puck was going."

"Right! But think about the kayaker too."

"Okay... so he wasn't prepared... so he was relying on luck?"

"Correct! Do you think the kayaker will try that again?"

"Doubtful. After going down the river without a paddle the first time, how would he know he could do it again without a paddle and still be okay?"

Granddaddy nodded his approval. "You know, I wasn't as smart as you are when I was your age, but I'm 76 years old today, and I'm here because every secret Colonel Reynolds shared with me was filled with truth. Every time I figured out how to apply one of the secrets he shared with me to my life, my life got better. I am living proof of a happy person who has lived by a few simple principles while still leading a fulfilling, meaningful, and success filled life. I want that for you too. I don't want you to ever doubt your ability to make things happen, but the hard truth is that I can only tell you about these secrets. I can't make you believe in them or use them."

It was still raining. We both stared out into the storm and saw a group of people running towards the parking lot. We stood and waved our arms and yelled, but they didn't seem to see or hear us. It was too bad because they still had a long way to go to get to the parking lot.

Watching them run past us got me thinking. This pavilion wasn't a fancy shelter, but it was keeping us safe and secure and that was all we really needed. The picnic table was in rough shape too, all scratched up from where kids had carved their names into it, but it was enough.

Those people were running to escape the storm and they were running in the only direction they knew. They didn't stop or look around for any other possibilities. If they'd been looking around, they might have seen the pavilion and been able to get out of the rain, but none of them did. They just ran with their heads down, trying to escape the rain. I wondered where they'd run to if they were trying to escape one of life's storms. Would they rely on luck to help them? Would they be happy when they arrived at their destination? Would it be enough?

6

Pops or Dad?

"The final forming of a person's character lies in their own hands."

- Anne Frank

I stared out into the storm mulling over the secrets Granddaddy was sharing with me. I don't know for how long, but then Granddaddy snapped me out of my trance. I turned towards him, not sure I'd heard him correctly. "What?"

"How's your dad doing?" Granddaddy repeated.

"You mean *Pops*?" I said, barely able to keep a tone of resentment out of my voice.

"Yeah, your father... How is he?" Granddaddy asked.

I could feel my lips pressing together. Why did Granddaddy have to bring him up? Up to this point we'd been having a nice talk. It was great listening to him and learning his secrets, but now he wanted to talk about someone I'd grown to hate. I didn't want to talk about Pops. What was I supposed to say anyway? Was I supposed to tell Granddaddy the truth? Did he really want to hear about all the times I'd been beaten—that we'd all been beaten?

Instead of answering, I shrugged. I could feel the weight of his stare pressing me for an answer, but I continued to stare at the floor. I remember reading somewhere that our eyes are a window to our soul, and I didn't want Granddaddy to look into my eyes and see how I really felt. After all, Pops was his son. I figured it might be hard for him to hear about how bad of a father his son had turned out to be. I didn't want to be reminded either.

Then I wondered why I was trying to spare Granddaddy's feelings. If he knew so much, then he must know how Pops turned out. And if Pops is his son... well then how could he have let it all happen? How could he not know about the years of pain his son had caused his family?

Granddaddy finally broke the silence. "I know I haven't been around a lot."

"No, you haven't," I said finally finding my voice.

"And maybe you'll say that because I haven't been around much it's none of my business, but I've always wondered why you call your father Pops? Every other father in our family is called Dad. Why do you call your dad Pops?"

"I don't know," I said shrugging again.

"Well, wouldn't you like to know?"

"I don't know.... What difference does it make?"

"Maybe it doesn't make any difference, but let me put it to you this way then. Why don't you call him Dad?"

I could feel the anger bubbling up inside me. I knew

exactly why I didn't call him Dad.

Granddaddy continued to question me. "I think you have a pretty good idea of why. What concerns me is that we can't talk about it. As long as you continue to ignore those reasons, or to examine them so you can understand them, they will continue to have influence over you and your life. Is that what you want?"

"No! And let's be clear, Pops doesn't have any influence over my life. I am nothing like him and I'll never be anything like him." I stopped abruptly, my heart starting to race. I might not give two cents for what Pops thought about anything, but I did care about what Granddaddy would think if I kept going.

"I know that. And we aren't here to talk about him," Granddaddy said. "I have to confess I had an ulterior motive for asking you the question. I was trying to figure out how your relationship with him was going. I guess I got part of the answer. Your relationship with your father isn't any better. But you still haven't told me why you call him Pops instead of Dad."

I looked at him with my mouth wide open. "So you don't actually care how he's doing? You were just tricking me with a question?"

Granddaddy's expression turned serious. "No, like I said before, I'm not here to trick you into anything. But we have a limited amount of time to talk, so I want to make sure that what we do talk about is meaningful. I don't want you to have to wait years for some of these lessons to make sense. I understood many of the lessons Colonel Reynolds shared with me, and was able to start applying some of them immediately. Others though, took me years to figure out. Some I figured out way too late… like how to be a "Dad" to your father."

And then I blurted it out in a rush, "Because he's not my Dad!"

Granddaddy looked surprised. "Now wait a minute. I was there when you were born and I can assure you that he's your Dad."

I shook my head defiantly. "No, you don't get what I mean. I know he's my father, but he's not my dad. A real dad would never treat his sons the way Pops treated me and my brother."

Granddaddy was nodding his head while staring at the floor.

"Like you said," I said trying to stay calm. "You haven't been around. You don't know what it's been like watching that meanness change my brother. He's just as mean as Pops is now, and he's always in and out of jail. I just can't bring myself to call Pops something as nice as "Dad" or "Daddy"! It feels like a lie. "Pops" is more neutral and unemotional. It's less endearing."

I took a deep breath trying to get away from the emotions that were getting in the way of me being able to stay calm. I hoped that if I stopped talking Granddaddy would break the silence, but he waited for me to keep going.

"Calling him Pops allows me to be civil with him when we interact. Maybe it isn't strictly true, but it helps me cope and get through it all, day after day. Calling him Dad would be a constant reminder of what he isn't, of who he'll never be, and of all the things I'll never be able to count on him for. That's why I don't let myself think of him as a real dad. He's not a real dad—at least not the kind of dad I wished I had. He's just Pops and I hope you're not expecting me to start calling him Dad.

"Nope.... No expectation of that."

I breathed a sigh of relief and wiped my sweaty palms on my pants. I hadn't realized how fired up I'd gotten and now I felt really self-conscious about all the things I'd just said. I'd never told anyone that before—maybe not even myself. It was beginning to feel like Granddaddy was putting me through the ringer, but I was willing to look at a few truths if it meant hearing the secrets he was sharing.

I remembered a teacher once saying that "to reveal is to heal" and I wondered if this was what he'd meant. Usually, I ignored my emotions and tried not to think too deeply about myself or the impact my surroundings have had on me. Instead, I'd learned to keep my emotions in check and not to let my weaknesses show. That went double when it came to Pops. There was no way I would ever be weak when it came to Pops.

"There is one thing I'd like you to consider though," Granddaddy said. "There are a lot of people who call their fathers Pops and it has the same meaning to them as the name Dad has to you. Calling him Pops instead of Dad won't change who he is, but it might influence the way you look at other fathers. And the truth is, you can't escape the reality of who he is by calling him by a different name."

I could feel my anger building, my blood pumping. I could call him anything I wanted to and no one, not even Granddaddy, could change that.

"Do you know why I started lifting weights?" I asked. "I started lifting weights and wrestling so I would be strong enough to beat Pops up so he'd stop beating on us. I knew Mom couldn't stop him, and the police never did anything about it, so I figured I'd have to. I decided I was going to do whatever it took to get strong enough to force him to stop. But my brother beat me to it.

"Pops started wailing on him one day and he exploded like a trapped animal. He beat the heck out of Pops like I've never seen a person get beat before. I guess my big brother just couldn't take another night of the beatings. Things changed after that. After Pops' wounds healed, he tried to beat us a few more times before he figured out my brother was now the enforcer in our house.

"Unfortunately, my brother wasn't the same after that. It was like all of Pops' violence had rubbed off on him. Now he's always angry and so mean that he's ready to fight anybody who tells him what to do... including the police. Now he's in and out of jail like it has a revolving door. I still get so angry when I think about it. It was like he never had a chance."

"I'm really sorry that happened to your brother... and to you," Granddaddy said. When he continued, his voice was quiet and thoughtful. "A very wise man, Mohammed the Prophet said: "He is not strong and powerful who throweth people down, but he is strong who holdeth himself from anger.""

I shook my head. "Don't worry," I said sarcastically. "I'm not going to throw your son down. I'll just keep calling him Pops. I'll keep my distance from him and I'll act civil towards him whether he deserves it or not." I was trying to sound calm, but without realizing I was doing it, I slammed my hand down on the picnic table hard enough to make it vibrate.

"Okay," he said. "I get that, and I know this is a tough subject, but I think you only heard the first part of what I said. You didn't hear the second part... "but he is strong who holdeth himself from anger". On your high school wrestling team you get rewarded for throwing people down, but in the real world there's no reward for throwing people down, even if you believe they deserve it. You saw what happened to your brother when he retaliated on your father and how it changed him. It didn't help him become a better person. What I hope you can see is that in your own way, you're doing the same thing only instead of wrestling your father to the ground to make your point, you're calling him Pops instead of Dad."

I didn't want to, but I could feel the truth of what he was saying. "I... I can't. I just can't call him Dad... I can't."

Granddaddy put a hand on my shoulder. "I understand, and I don't expect you to call him Dad... He'd probably freak out if you did anyway. All I want you to think about is all the energy it's costing you to keep him in his place by calling him Pops. I'm willing to bet that every time you say it you feel a spike in anger. Do you want to feel that for the rest of your life? Will it be worth it if you end up carrying that anger around with you for the rest of your life? Please trust me when I say this, if you do, you will live to regret it."

And then he was quiet. Maybe Granddaddy had sensed he'd pushed me as far as he could with this subject. I wondered if I was stuck in a bizarre rerun of *Colombo*, the police detective show from the '70s we used to watch when we were growing up. Columbo was definitely a cool detective. He had a real talent for getting people to tell him what he wanted to know. He would emotionally push his suspects to the edge with his questions, get some information out of them, and then pull back just short of sending his suspects into a rage.

I suddenly wondered if that was Granddaddy's plan—to pull a "Columbo" on me. He had managed to get me to say a whole lot of things I would have never said voluntarily. He'd also gotten me to talk and think about the whole Pops thing without ever actually forcing me. Now he was tactically retreating. Was that his goal all along? If it was, he'd been successful. He'd shaken my beliefs, deftly planted a seed in my head about Pops and about not throwing people down in the real world, and then skillfully he'd stopped just short of me turning into a violent storm.

"Do you know who Socrates was?" Granddaddy asked breaking the silence.

Once again, Granddaddy had caught me off guard and I had to think about it for a minute. Yes, I did know who Socrates was. "Sure."

"Well, Socrates said a lot of things we still talk about today. What I like about Socrates is that if we're still talking about the things he was talking about thousands of years ago, then there's probably something to it... It means we aren't the first people to face these problems in our lives."

"Hmm," I mused. "I never thought about it like that. Do you think Socrates had issues with his dad too?"

Granddaddy chuckled. "I don't know... maybe. If he did though, he must have come through them okay because he left us with some really great ideas to help us get past our problems. One of those ideas is that "an unexamined life isn't worth living." This is something we all need to do—we need to get to know ourselves and understand why we do the things we do. Lazy people don't do this. Neither do people who are afraid. Instead, they live their lives doing the same things over and over again because they haven't been able to find the courage to ask themselves the hard questions."

I nodded my head agreeing with him. Talking about Pops was definitely hard, but I wasn't going to avoid it because I was afraid.

"That's one of the reasons I wanted to talk to you about your father. I wanted to help you figure out if you're ready to start taking the time to get to know yourself and understand why you do things. And I'm not saying there's a right or wrong answer here. There isn't. What I can tell you is that when you take the time to understand yourself, the quality of your life will improve dramatically. You'll be much more likely to live a life filled with things you chose to do rather than living a life where all you do is react to the things other people do."

I winced. Up to this point I thought I'd known why I did everything. I had a plan. I had a focus. Did I understand why? All this revealing was definitely not healing. Instead, it felt more like my feet had been knocked out from beneath me and I was heading face first for the mat.

"Listen kid, I know how hard some of this stuff is to talk about, but I promise it will make more sense as we go along. Examining your life isn't just about looking at the tough stuff. It's about looking at the good stuff too. All the stuff we've already talked about—like your plans and goals. All that stuff proves you're moving in a good direction. You're taking steps most grown men have never even considered and I'm really impressed by it."

I laughed. "Well I'm glad I got something right!"

"Oh come on now. Like I said, you've gotten a lot of things right."

"I don't know. Sometimes I feel so out of place it's really frustrating. It's not like there's anybody around who can relate to what I'm doing.... Maybe I was born in the wrong generation. Maybe I should have been born when I could have been a part of your generation. Then I could have used my ability to fight for something good like fighting Hitler and making the world a better place to live—like you did."

"I guess you can look at it like that, but it won't change the fact that you're living now. Besides, you can do great things here just as easily. You already are."

I shrugged my shoulders and pondered what he'd said. I did have my sports and instead of using all my strength, skills, and ability to defend myself against Pops, I was now using them to excel in the weight room, on the football field, and on the wrestling mat. But would I have any of it if my big brother hadn't stepped up?

"Maybe," I started, "but that wasn't my original plan. My first plan was to get strong enough to stop Pops. My brother just beat me to it. It was like he sacrificed himself for my mom and me. I didn't know he was going to do it, and I felt bad because he changed after that. Maybe if I could have helped him, things would've worked out differently for him."

"I can understand how you'd feel like that. It goes along with what you said about feeling like you might have been better off using your skills to help fight Hitler. It would have been different if you and your brother had been fighting side by side for something you both believed in. But I can just about guarantee that if you asked him if he would have wanted you to be a part of what happened, he'd say no."

"You think so?" I asked hopefully.

"Absolutely. That's why people step up and join the military or become leaders in the first place. They want to clear the path of opportunity for others. I can tell you with absolute certainty that he's proud of you even if he's never said it. And even though your relationship with him has changed, everything you achieve is evidence to him that what he did had value. Something good came out of a very bad situation."

"You really think he feels that way?"

Granddaddy nodded.

I thought about that for a minute. "But we hardly ever talk."

"Families are tough sometimes. Maybe the best way you can honor his effort is by being grateful for both him and the path he cleared for you."

"I never would have thought of it like that. I've always felt guilty."

"Trust me, that's not what your brother wants either. That's not what people who pave the way want. It's certainly not what any soldier wants. All they want is for you to succeed."

"You know, when I realized I wasn't going to have to stop Pops, that was when I took all my intensity and started putting it all into sports instead. I guess you're right. If it hadn't been for my brother, I might not have made it this far."

Granddaddy nodded his head in agreement. "We all like to think our accomplishments are the result of our hard work and effort... and that's true, but it's also true that no one ever accomplishes anything without the aide and assistance of other people along the way. It's unfortunate that sometimes that aide and assistance is the result of a bad situation."

7

Every Tragedy Includes an Opportunity

"When we meet real tragedy in life, we can react in two ways - either by losing hope and falling into self-destructive habits, or by using the challenge to find our inner strength. Thanks to the teachings of Buddha, I have been able to take this second way."

- Dalai Lama

We were quiet again; the rain still coming down. I took a deep breath trying to smell the storm. I couldn't decide if what I smelled was what a storm was supposed to smell like, but it smelled good all the same.

I wondered what Granddaddy was thinking about me. I was telling him stuff I never thought I'd say out loud to anyone. It felt strange because I've barely seen him over the years and hardly know him, but I still felt completely at ease with him.

"You know," Granddaddy said breaking the silence, "it takes a lot of courage to come through hard times. And I don't only mean the kind of courage that helps you make a touchdown or pin someone to the mat. You didn't crumple under the weight of what you went through. Instead you began working out and reading books. You searched for solutions to your unfortunate circumstances and found things to do to give yourself hope. You didn't give up on yourself! You didn't follow the footsteps of violence you found in your home and in the streets. You turned a terrible, negative environment into a powerful motivational force. Call it pay-back if you wish, but you decided that someday you would be the real-deal, and that no one would be able to hold you down on the wrestling mat or in the real world."

I nodded my head.

"I'm serious. History is filled with the names of successful people who grew up without the benefit of having someone standing nearby and cheering them on to victory. For example, when Napoleon was a little boy attending a military academy, one of his teachers made his life miserable."

"Really?" I said surprised.

"Later, it was said that on his death bed, Napoleon said, "I wonder what my old teacher thinks of me now?" I'd be willing to bet Napoleon also thought about what his teacher had said when his plans were executed to a victorious conclusion. And Napoleon is just one example of a reoccurring pattern throughout history, right up to today. Do you know who Michael Phelps is?"

"Sure," I replied. "He's an Olympic swimmer who represented the United States and won 18 gold medals between the 2008 and 2012 summer Olympics."

"I'm not surprised you know that. Did you know that when a reporter asked him what drove him to be so successful, he said a teacher had once told him he'd never be successful? I guess he proved that teacher wrong.

"The Roman Emperor Marcus Aurelius said, "A man's greatest tragedies usually lead to a man's greatest successes". Knowing what those great men thought, I have to wonder how many of your victories were motivated by a desire to prove to everyone, including your father, that you could do it. That you weren't ever going to let anyone stop you from pursuing your goals without a fair fight."

I liked that Granddaddy said a "fair" fight. That was important to me. I was always aware of how strong I was and how easy it would be to push people around or intimidate them. At least with sports I can be strong without being considered a bully. If things had gone differently at home, that might have happened. But with sports, I don't have to think about what might have happened. I can be as strong and as skilled as I set my mind to be because it's always a fair fight. It's always a situation where I start out equal with my competition.

"You see," Granddaddy continued, "you have, in a strange sort of way, taken advantage of a gift many people are never aware of. You've taken the chaos and struggles you've experienced in your life and used them as inspiration to do and be more. You could have chosen to give up, but you didn't. Instead, you started designing your life for success and now your desire to succeed in life is a part of who you are. It's etched into your soul."

"My girlfriend is always saying that when life gives you lemons, you make lemonade."

"She's right! And it's good to remember your roots. We all start somewhere and it doesn't do any good to fret about it after the fact. At that point, it's a history of factual events that took place. But that's when each of us gets to start asking better questions. What did ***I*** learn from the chaos of my past experience? How can ***I*** use my past experience to help me succeed in the future? How can ***I*** succeed in a way that makes the world better without falling under the weight of all the chaos around me?"

Granddaddy turned and looked at me. "You could have simply busied yourself with collecting trophies and medals. But again, you didn't. Maybe now's as good a time as any for you to acknowledge that you chose a different kind of future for yourself. You've experienced great tragedies, but now you've made a whole series of better choices and decisions, and have been preparing yourself for success as a result. Your life has purpose now, and once you have a purpose and a plan... well... those are the roots of a meaningful life."

"You think I have a purpose?" I asked. "I've had people say things like that to me. Some people tell me I was born to wrestle, but I don't know. What do you think?"

"No one can tell you what you were born to do. That's something you get to decide as you set out on your own personal journey. Whatever you are focusing on at any given moment in time is your purpose in that moment. The more you learn about yourself, the easier it becomes to make decisions about what to do next. Right now, your past is a reminder of what you don't want. But as you continue pursuing your goals, your past will start filling up with things you feel good about too."

Granddaddy turned to look at me. "This might sound like a weird question, but do you ever feel grateful for what you've accomplished?"

"What, like when I win at wrestling or get a good grade?"

"Kind of. Those are definitely things to be grateful for, but I was thinking more along the lines of being grateful to people who have helped you along the way."

"Sure. I'm grateful for my girlfriend and my coaches I guess. It feels kind of weird to think about being grateful. I haven't thought about it like that before."

"People get confused about what it means to be grateful. Being grateful doesn't mean you owe somebody for something they did for you. Like if someone helped you finish your yard work so you could go out and do something else. It's more like you understand that if it weren't for what someone else did, you might not be where you are. No one makes it on their own. The more we understand that, the more likely we are to feel gratitude for the people who've helped us succeed, whether or not they are aware of the part they played in our success, even when it feels like they don't deserve it."

I shook my head. "You're talking about Pops again, right?"

"Maybe. Give it a shot. See if you can come up with a reason to be grateful when it comes to your father."

I sighed. "Okay. First of all, I hope you're not expecting me to be grateful for what he did."

"Nope."

"Good." I tried to think of why I would be grateful for him, but I was having trouble.

After a couple of minutes, Granddaddy broke the silence. "Don't focus on what he did or didn't do."

"What else is there to focus on?" I asked.

"You tell me."

If I took all the beatings out of the picture, there wasn't much left. I didn't really know Pops any other way. The only other thing he did for me was to help create me. I groaned. "I got it. He helped make me. I wouldn't be here if it weren't for him."

Granddaddy smiled. "That's definitely something to be grateful for. One of the reasons you're here, right now, sharing all these secrets with me, is because of your father. I can honestly say *I'm* grateful for that. Let me ask you a different question. How do you feel about yourself as a person?"

"Okay... that's a weird question. I'm not conceited or anything like that... at least I don't think I am."

"From what I've seen, you aren't conceited or self-centered. But think about your strengths too. Think about what you've accomplished so far even with all the bad stuff you've experienced. You're strong, you have a good work ethic, you don't quit when things get tough, and you know how to work through things even when they're tough to get through."

"I try to do those things for sure," I said trying not to sound as puffed up as what Granddaddy was saying about me was making me feel.

"Now, I don't know if your father has any of those traits, but your life might not be going in such a good direction if it had been different... if it had been easier. All your strengths and abilities have developed the way they have as a result of the way you've grown up so far. If you'd been a different kind of person, you might have ended up like other people who've experienced the same kinds of hardships as you have. People who spend their time complaining about how bad their life is while never wondering if they could build a better life. They don't look for things to be grateful for, so they never find them.

"Every success you've experienced has its roots in your past. Every good thing you have in your life has its roots in your past. You may not like your past, or the people in your past, but you wouldn't be here, right now, if it weren't for your past."

"You're killing me here," I said. "I've spent my whole life doing everything I could to stay away from everything you're talking about—including Pops. But now... and I get that I can be grateful that he helped make me, but I'm still not talking to him. I'm not going to run home and thank him."

"That's fine. I wouldn't expect you to. But I'll warn you right now, gratitude has a way of sneaking up on you. And now that we've been talking about it, you're going to start seeing some of the people in your life differently. That's what happened with me and my father."

"What?" I asked. "Really?"

"It's like I told you, I ran away when I was 16 to join the military. I had to get away from my father too. But years later, after I started to truly understand the power of gratitude, it was easier for me to think about him. And then I discovered something really interesting about gratitude. It doesn't take anywhere near as much energy to be grateful and forgiving as it does to keep your distance and to constantly have your guard up."

"You should have told me to bring a notebook. I don't know how I'm going to remember all this stuff!"

"Don't worry. You won't need to write it down. These secrets are the kind of stuff you won't forget. But you're right, we have been going through a lot of stuff. How are you doing with all this talking?"

"Well... it's definitely weird looking back at things because now they feel different... like the whole situation with my brother. I'm guessing that after I think about him for a while I'm going to be grateful for him too." I shook my head in complete disbelief at what was going on inside my head. But somehow I knew it was going to be okay. I looked at Granddaddy and smiled. "I'm doing okay."

8

What's in a Name?

"He who does not trust enough, will not be trusted."

- Lao Tzu

"I'm glad to hear it because I have another question to ask you."

"I hope it's an easy one," I groaned.

"The first time you ask yourself any question, it can be a bit of a struggle. Sometimes the questions we need to answer make us squirm because they force us to look a little deeper. So I can't promise this question is going to be any easier than the last, but if you want me to stop. I will."

"NO!" I shouted and then immediately calmed my voice down. "No. I want to keep going. Ask me."

"I'd like to know why you don't ever call anybody by their name."

"What? I don't understand."

"Like I told you before, I've been around even though you weren't aware of it." Granddaddy leaned towards me like he didn't want anybody else to hear what he was going to say next. "Part of my military training included learning how to blend into my surroundings without people noticing me."

"I don't get it. Why didn't you want me to know you were there?" I said.

"That's a very complicated question to answer, and I hope you'll find it within yourself to trust me when I say that it was always for your own benefit. Can you do that?"

I hesitated because I really did want to know, but then I shrugged. "I guess so."

"Good... now back to the question I asked. Do you know that in all the times I've heard you talking with people, I've never ever heard you call anybody by their name? You always refer to people by their relationship to you."

I frowned. "I don't do that."

Granddaddy nodded his head. "Yes, you do, and it worries me. For example, you've been dating the same girl for a year now, so I'm figuring she's one of the most important people in your life, and yet you always refer to her as "my girlfriend". That's how you've referred to her today—as your girlfriend. You haven't said her name once."

I sat and thought about what he was saying. Was he right? Maybe he was right. Maybe I didn't call people by their names. It seemed like a crazy thing to do because I know how much I enjoyed hearing my name, especially when it was for something like scoring a touchdown or a pin. I loved it!

Then I remembered a stupid etiquette class I'd sat through as a freshman where the teacher had said that we should always try to use people's names when we talk to them. It was a sign of respect. Rats! Now Granddaddy was going to expect me to be able to explain why I was doing this.

"Oh boy!" I sighed heavily. "Here comes the pain of getting to know myself again. Well, here goes nothing! Maybe I do it to protect myself?"

"Are you asking me a question or telling me why you do it?"

"I'm not really sure. I've never thought about it before. Give me a minute."

"Take all the time you need," Granddaddy said.

I thought about the people we'd been talking about. He was right. It was always "my girlfriend" or "my big brother" or "one of my teammates," but I was stuck. I couldn't come up with a reason. "I give up. Tell me why," I said.

"You think I know?" Granddaddy laughed. "I don't know why—only you know why. The thing I know is that people very often start doing something a certain way and then they keep doing it the same way until they come up with a better reason not to do it. So maybe you started referring to one person like this, it became a habit, and you started doing it with everyone."

"You think it's because I started calling Pops *Pops* instead of Dad, don't you."

Granddaddy shrugged.

I shook my head. "Look, I know you say you've been around, but being at my football games and wrestling matches isn't the same as being in my house. It's different there, and I had to do what I had to do to keep my distance from him. I had to protect myself and that was one of the ways I did it—by calling him Pops. I should have been able to trust him, to rely on him, and I couldn't."

I could feel my throat getting tight and took a few seconds to regain my control. "I had to do things to stop myself from hoping he'd ever change. It wasn't going to happen. As long as I call him Pops, I won't forget what he's really like or that he's not a good dad, and then he won't be able to hurt me anymore than he already has."

"I can understand that. It makes a lot of sense." Granddaddy waited a bit before continuing. "Is there any possibility you don't call other people by their names because you're afraid they might betray you too? The way your father did?"

"I don't know... maybe," I said, a hint of a whine entering my voice. "Can't you just tell me what you think?"

"Look," Granddaddy continued, "every reason you do something isn't automatically a bad reason. I understand why you call your father Pops. And you came up with the idea that you might be doing it with other people as a way of protecting yourself."

"I know, but do you think that's why I'm doing it?" I asked.

"Let's look at it. You call your father Pops to protect yourself from him. And like I said, people tend to do the same things over and over again, so yeah, I think it's possible you don't refer to people by name as a way of protecting yourself."

"It makes sense... I think."

"I also said people can change when they have a really good reason. So let me ask you. Do you think your girlfriend is going to betray you?"

"No!" I answered emphatically.

"I agree with you. I don't think she will either," Granddaddy answered. "But trust is a two way street. If you don't trust and respect her enough to talk about her using her name, how does she know she can trust and respect you?"

"I never thought about it that way," I said shaking my head.

"Using someone's name is a sign of respect. It feels good when people say your name. I'm sure you can relate to that. I've heard your name over the loudspeaker plenty of times and I've seen you smile when you hear it."

I looked down trying to hide the smile on my face. He was right. I liked it a lot.

"It's too soon to tell if she's the girl you're going to stick with, but if she is, she'll be there to protect you too. She'll even protect you from yourself when it's necessary! That alone should earn your respect. You know, I probably wouldn't have achieved anywhere near as much as I have if it wasn't for your Grandmother. I know she seems like the quiet passive type, but believe me, she's every bit as strong as I am. Granted, she can't lift as much weight as I can, but she is stronger than I could ever be in so many ways. I owe everything to her."

"Wow, I never knew," I replied.

"She sees and hears things I miss. She's great at reading people's faces. She has a tremendous amount of patience, which she's needed living with me, but she's never done or said anything that wasn't in my best interest. She's picked me up when I've fallen and redirected me when I've lost my way. She's also protected me from myself, especially when I was blind to the obvious. Like your girlfriend, she too, occasionally fumbles through her purse looking for her keys... and I agree with you, it's cute. I love your grandmother with all my heart."

Granddaddy sat with a smile on his face and looked like he was lost in thought. Then he cleared his throat and continued. "I don't know if your girlfriend will turn out to be your lifelong love, but I can tell you that your relationship will only grow as far as your trust and respect for her will allow. If you don't trust her enough to open up and be your whole self around her, then you'll never know if she's the right one or not. Just as important though, is for you to trust yourself enough to let her be her whole self with you. People are a lot like puzzles when it comes to love. We each have a whole lot of pieces, but when they fit together, we can create something really great."

"I get what you're saying, but what happens if I trust her and it turns out she's not the right one?"

"There are a couple of ways to answer that. One is with the phrase: *nothing ventured nothing gained*. The other is with the phrase: *with great risk comes great reward*."

"I've heard both of those."

Granddaddy nodded his approval. "Okay. Then I don't have to explain that this is one of those times when you get to decide how you want to proceed. Will you settle for what you've got? Or will you reach for something better?"

I thought about it for a couple of seconds and quietly said, "Her name is Jenn." I was surprised at how it felt to say that. It felt really good. Then I turned to Granddaddy feeling the smile on my own face. "My girlfriend's name is Jenn."

9

Attitude of Gratitude

"Reflect upon your present blessings, of which every man has plenty; not on your past misfortunes, of which all men have some."

- Charles Dickens

"Her name is Jenn," Granddaddy said turning and smiling at me. "Thanks for sharing her name with me."

"You're welcome." I responded.

"Of course I have to confess that I already knew her name," he said.

"Yeah. I kinda figured you did."

"But thank you anyway," He said. "Thank you for finally trusting me enough to share her name with me. That's another step towards your Kaizen."

"My Kai... what?" I asked with a confused look on my face.

"Don't worry about that right now. We'll get to it soon enough. First though, I want to talk about what I did after you told me Jenn's name."

"Okay," I said a little unsure of what Granddaddy was talking about.

"What did I do after you told me Jenn's name?" Granddaddy asked.

"I don't know," I replied with a shrug. "Did you do something?"

"Sure I did," Granddaddy said. "The problem is that what I did is so simple that most people would miss it simply because they aren't paying attention. But I'm willing to bet that if you take a minute, you'll remember. Think about it. You turned to me with a big smile on your face and said, "My girlfriend's name is Jenn". Then I...."

"I don't remember you doing anything specific. Maybe you turned towards me a little and smiled? Is that what you're talking about?"

"You're getting close, and you're definitely good at observing people's physical movements, but I did more than turn towards you and smile. In some ways, I'm not surprised you didn't catch it. You probably don't experience what I did on a daily basis."

"Well, if I don't know what it is, how can I tell you what it is?" I asked.

Sensing my frustration, Granddaddy calmly said, "I wouldn't be asking the question if I wasn't sure you already knew the answer. You do know. You just don't know you know."

I shook my head. I didn't want to disagree with him, but I honestly didn't know what he expected me to say.

Granddaddy continued. "I know how it sounds, but psychologically speaking, even though your conscious mind has already moved on and is paying attention to what I'm saying right now, your subconscious mind recorded and stored what happened. It did that for you because it knows your conscious mind can only pay attention to so many things in any given moment, usually seven things—plus or minus a couple. Your subconscious mind on the other hand is limitless. It never misses a thing. It's like a 360 degree movie camera that's always running; only there's no director telling it what to record. Instead, it records everything it witnesses. To access it, all you have to do is find a way to play back the recording."

I had an idea. "We learned about hypnosis in one of my classes. Is that what you're talking about?"

"Hypnosis is definitely one of the ways people can gain access to what's been stored in their subconscious mind, but in a situation like this one, where I'm asking you to tell me about something that happened a couple of minutes ago, it's not really necessary. But getting yourself into the right state of mind will help. It's a pretty basic psychological tactic. Want to try it?"

"Sure.... So... you're not going to hypnotize me?"

Granddaddy chuckled. "Let's try this first."

"Okay, but could you hypnotize me if you wanted to?" I asked eagerly.

"Probably," Granddaddy said with a mischievous smile. "Okay... Take a deep breath and let it out slowly." The tone of his voice was changing as he spoke becoming calmer and slower. "Close your eyes... relax... and take another deep breath... slowly letting it out."

I followed his instructions and felt myself relaxing.

"Listen to the rain... You've been hearing it since we sat down... the steady pitter-patter of it hitting the roof above us. Feel the cool air as it blows through the pavilion carrying light drops of rain along with it. We don't mind the rain though because we're enjoying the conversation. I was telling you about how much your Grandmother means to me. You thought about it and decided to tell me your girlfriend's name. You turned to me with a smile and said "My girlfriend's name in Jenn"... then I... " Granddaddy let his voice trail off.

"Then you turned towards me... and smiled... and said thanks?" I opened my eyes and looked at Granddaddy. "Did I get it right? Is that what you said?"

"Very good. I did say thanks. Actually I said "Thanks for telling me her name was Jenn", but you got the part I was hoping you would. You remembered that I said thanks. Like I said, it was a very simple thing, but sometimes the simplest things are the toughest to grab a hold of.

"I also told you that you already knew the answer. The reason I wanted you to remember it on your own was partly because I wanted to prove to you that you could, but I also wanted you to remember what it felt like to hear me express my gratitude for sharing Jenn's name with me. Thanks and thank you are very powerful words. I made it even more powerful by clearly directing my thanks right to you when I turned and smiled. I also looked you right in the eye when I said it."

"Yeah, I remember that part now. Maybe that's why I was having a hard time remembering it. It felt a little weird actually."

"I get that. It's tough for a guy your age to think about making eye contact. It isn't always safe to do it in the streets. I bet you do it when you're sizing up your competition in sports though."

"Sure do. I'm not afraid of the competition and I want to make sure they know it."

"Did you know that studies show that it's not what you say, but rather "how" you say it that counts for about 55% of what a person notices and then feels about you?" Granddaddy asked. "That's what you're doing when you look your competition in the eye. You're showing them you're confident. That's 100% body language. When I said thanks, I used my body language in addition to my words as another way of making sure you knew I was genuinely grateful."

"I didn't realize I was using body language like that."

"We're always using our body language. Once you start paying attention to other people's body language, you'll be amazed at what you learn. It goes back to the whole thing I was saying about your subconscious. Even when you aren't paying attention, your subconscious mind will step in and pay attention for you. So you're already reading and reacting to people's body language, but right now it's mostly with your subconscious mind. For example, I bet you know what kind of mood Jenn is in without her having to say anything."

"Well... yes and no. I can tell when she's in a mood. I just don't always know why."

Granddaddy laughed. "Yes, but you can tell something is going on. I bet she can read your body language too. You can do a lot with body language—especially because most people aren't paying attention. Instead, their subconscious mind is paying attention for them and they end up responding to someone's body language without even realizing they're doing it. You can actually use your body language to encourage people to trust you and treat you well. When you exude confidence and happiness and an attitude of gratitude, it will show and people will be more likely to like you, respect you, and want to be around you."

"Hmm," I murmured. "You sure do know a lot about people. I had no idea I was using my body language like that."

"Oh, trust me, you knew it. It was just so natural for you that you never realized it. See, we learn these kinds of things by steps. As soon as we master the first step, we're ready to take the next step. You've already had an introduction to some of the things we've been talking about. Today, you're achieving a deeper level of understanding for some of the ideas you've already been applying to your life. For example, you just learned more about how body language works while you were gaining a deeper understanding of gratitude and how important gratitude is. Each step you take will aide you as you move towards your Kaizen."

"You said that word again. Are you going to tell me what it is?"

"Yes. In time I'll explain it to you, but not right this minute," Granddaddy replied. "First, I have something else I'd like to share about gratitude."

"I get it Granddaddy. Be grateful," I said, impatient to talk about something more interesting.

"You understand one aspect of gratitude. But understanding gratitude is like understanding anything else. It's a step by step process. When you were growing up, you learned how to crawl first, then you learned how to walk, and before you knew it, you were running. But you didn't start with running. You started with crawling and built up to it. Understanding the secrets we're talking about today works the same way. You'll understand the general idea, but as you learn more, you'll be taking bigger steps. Each step successfully taken gives you confidence to take the next step—even if you fail. Have you ever watched a toddler trying to stand and walk the first few times?"

"Yeah, my girlfriend...I mean *Jenn,* is an aunt and we watched her niece trying to walk one day. It was pretty funny. She fell a lot."

"Maybe so, but did she quit?"

I shook my head no.

"Of course she didn't. If she had, she wouldn't be walking now. She didn't stop after each fall and think to herself 'I'm never going to master this, it's too hard!' Instead, she kept right on working at it. Too many people take one step, fail, and then never find the courage to try taking another step. They've forgotten what it was like to be two years old and fearless. Instead, they're afraid people will think they're stupid for trying something new. Or they're too proud to let other people see them struggle. Or they're too concerned about what people will think of them if they fail. People waste a lot of time and a lot of life when they give into those excuses. We all make mistakes and fail along the way, but when we do, we can use that information to increase our chances of succeeding when we're ready to try again."

"I get the whole crawl before you can walk thing, but how can I fail with gratitude? I already know how to say thank you."

"And it's easy enough to say thank you," Granddaddy said. "But that's only one part—one step. The next step is to realize that we are surrounded by things to be grateful for, every minute of every day. Remember when you asked me about my house and my car?"

I nodded.

"I'm grateful for both of them. They may not seem extraordinary to your eyes, but to mine, they provide comfort and shelter and a sense of security for me and your grandmother. We're grateful for what we have and don't need or desire more than what we have. Sometimes, people who are always thinking about buying a bigger house or car haven't stopped to consider whether or not they're grateful for what they already have. If they did stop to feel grateful, they'd also have to stop and ask themselves why they want more. The point is, if you move forward with the idea that you're always on the lookout for more ways to experience gratitude, you'll never run out of reasons, people, or things to be grateful for."

I gave him a skeptical look.

Granddaddy nodded. "Okay, let me try to explain what gratitude really feels like."

I watched him close his eyes, take a deep breath, and smile to himself.

"When I start thinking about everything I'm grateful for, it fills me up to the point where I could explode with gratitude and happiness. Like sitting here and talking with you. I'm very grateful for this time, but I'm also extremely grateful for everything that led me here. What I want you to understand is that the only way I could be here is because my past led me here. And I wouldn't trade this time for anything."

Granddaddy opened his eyes and looked at me. "Don't get me wrong. I've had tough times too, just like everybody else. I just choose to learn from my mistakes and failures, and to be grateful for everything and everyone who's helped me along the way. When I look back at my life, I choose to remember the lessons I learned and all the situations that have provided me with opportunities to be grateful. I let go of the rest.

"As your understanding of the role gratitude plays in your life deepens, remember that no one accomplishes anything alone. Whenever you accomplish anything, you can start by being grateful for the knowledge and skill you used to make it happen, but make sure you start looking around too. As soon as you do, you'll quickly begin to realize how much help you've gotten along the way."

I thought about that and realized I knew exactly what he was talking about. "You mean like when I wrestle and I know my girlfriend's... sorry, I mean *Jenn's* there. I'm too focused to look her way, but knowing she's there makes a difference."

"I bet it does. The question is, do you say thank you to her for being there?"

That was a tough question, but not because I didn't know the answer. I did. "No... not really. I smile at her and I think she knows I'm glad she's there, but I don't think I've ever actually said the words."

Granddaddy was nodding his head and then asked, "How do you think she'd feel if you did?"

I couldn't help but smile. "Good."

"You're smiling thinking about it so I know you're getting it. Most people don't realize how great it feels to express their gratitude. If they did, they'd do it all the time because it's contagious. It's like tossing a tiny pebble into a lake. When the pebble hits the water, it starts a chain of reactions beginning with the first water molecules the pebble comes in contact with. Those molecules pass their reaction along to the next. We see the result as circular rings expanding and growing well beyond the point of impact, all from one tiny pebble."

"Wow." That was all I could say.

"Wow is right. It's almost like magic and yet most people miss it because they don't think in terms of gratitude. In fact, if someone genuinely expresses gratitude to them, they get uncomfortable. They don't even know how to react. Like you didn't when I said thanks for telling me Jenn's name. Gratitude can and will improve the quality of your life... if you let it. You don't have to start with grand gestures either. Simply start by looking for things to be grateful for. Once you get used to doing that, start figuring out how to express it."

I turned to Granddaddy and looked him right in the eye. "Thanks for being here today." It took every ounce of my strength to hold his gaze, but I did.

Granddaddy clapped a hand on my shoulder and with genuine warmth said, "You're welcome."

He was right. It felt really good. Strange, but really good.

10

Do the Work!

"A dream doesn't become reality through magic; it takes sweat, determination, and hard work."

- Collin Powell

"Granddaddy?" I started. "Can I ask you a question?"

"Of course."

"How do you remember all this stuff? It's like you know all these things. You talk about people I've barely ever heard of."

Granddaddy sighed and nodded. "I know it might sound like I know a lot, but you have to remember I'm a lot older than you. You also need to understand that I sought out knowledge too."

"You studied?"

"Kind of. But it's more like reading books about things and people that interested me. For example, we've been talking about gratitude. When I first heard the idea, I wanted to know more so I started doing a little research. Know what I found out?"

I shook my head no.

"I found out that a man named Cicero said that gratitude wasn't just the greatest of virtues, but that it was the parent of all other virtues. What's really amazing is that he said it over 2000 years ago. He lived before Jesus Christ."

"So you studied Cicero?"

"Yes. I decided I wanted to know more about him. He lived so long ago and yet the things he said were relevant to me. His ideas made sense to me and I liked the thought of having something in common with someone who lived so long ago. Just out of curiosity, have you heard of him or read about him in school?"

"Maybe. I think I remember his name from world history. Was he a Roman or something?"

Granddaddy chuckled. "Oh he was definitely a Roman, but he was a great speaker and today he's considered one of the most versatile minds to ever grace ancient Rome."

"Sorry. I guess I don't remember what we learned about him. But I'm pretty sure it didn't have anything to do with gratitude."

"I'm not surprised. Today's history books don't seem to contain much more than facts and dates. They tell the facts of what men and women did, but don't include the details about who they were as people. We don't get to read their stories, so we don't have enough information to know what they were thinking, or truly understand the reasons that inspired their actions.

"It's sad too because those people had struggles in their lives just like you and I have in ours. I always wonder how much more interested kids in school would be if they stopped to realize that every historical figure they're reading about was a teenager once upon a time too. Take Joan of Arc for example. She was 13 years old when she started having visions of driving the English out of France. When she was 16, she made her way to the French Royal Court and convinced the disinherited French crown prince, Charles of Valois, to let her lead his forces against the English. At 17, she won a series of battles and honored her promise to Charles of seeing him crowned king.

"We were just talking about Cicero. This amazing man was once the same age as you are right now. Wouldn't you love to know how he came up with all his great ideas? I wonder who he sat down and talked with. Was there someone like Colonel Reynolds in his life too?"

"Yeah... Or maybe he sat down and talked with his Granddaddy," I offered enthusiastically.

"Maybe," Granddaddy mused. "We can learn so much more from history than facts. It seems to me it's a challenge for students to get inspired by memorizing a bunch of dates."

"I can tell you from experience that dates aren't inspiring. They're boring. All they are is the difference between an A, a B, a C, or whatever." I looked at Granddaddy. "Do you think it will ever change?"

Granddaddy looked thoughtful. "I'd like to think it would. I'd like to think the people who write history books will figure out that most of us get inspired by people, not by the date and time those people did something. Take movies for example. There are a lot of historical movies that are historically accurate and really inspiring. The actors in those movies aren't talking about dates. They're showing us what else was going on during that time, and we get to live through those historical points in time with them.

"Movie makers know how to keep us interested. They tell us more about what was really going on with those people. Sometimes they help us see the good guys succeed and the bad guys fail. If a director has done a good job, we might even have learned a lesson, or have gotten some information that might help us avoid making mistakes in our own lives. A really good, historically accurate movie might even inspire us to do more with our lives."

"They should make a history class like that—all movies. That would be a great class and we'd get to know more about the people in the process," I said.

Granddaddy shrugged. "You might be right, but even if they talked about it, it's doubtful the decision makers would agree on which movies to show. There'd be too many opposing opinions. They'd disagree on how much information to give you, or about whether or not you have a right to hear both sides of a story. They'd argue about how much of the story you should be exposed to, and there'd be times when they'd make decisions believing you need to be protected from the whole truth.

"Those are just a few of the reasons why you only get the information you get right now... a lot of bare bones dates and facts rather than the whole story. I wish they'd give you more information. I think it'd be very powerful for young people to realize how young some of the greatest leaders the world has ever known were when they were making decisions that changed the course of history."

"It would be easier on the teachers too I bet," I said.

Granddaddy cocked his head to the side and looked at me.

I shrugged. "I've overheard teachers talking about how hard it is to keep up with all the things they have to do. They get stressed about all the testing, and then they stress us out with everything they expect us to learn. It's not like it's a secret."

"They do expect a lot from teachers these days. They expect them to stay inspired, and then expect them to inspire their students while following curriculum restrictions that limit what they can teach. But... that's a topic for another day. What I hope you will take away from this is that just because your teachers aren't able to dive into the details, that doesn't mean you can't.

"You have a choice. You can walk away from your classes satisfied with having learned enough information to pass your tests, or you can take notice of the people and events that sound interesting to you and check them out on your own. And not just in history class either. You'll hear about amazing people in your other classes too. Look at it this way, every person who made it into one of your school books has a story to tell. If the results sound interesting, no one's going to stop you from checking out the whole story on your own."

"Maybe, but doing more homework by choice?" I moaned. "I don't know."

Granddaddy laughed. "I'm not saying to check out every person you read about. Just take a minute to ask yourself how a regular person... someone like you... could end up where they ended up. If you realize you'd really like to know the answer, check them out. It's easy enough to do with the Internet."

I nodded. "I guess I could do that."

"Good. It's important to study successful people. The cool thing is that successful people want you to succeed too. They don't want you to struggle like they did. That's why their stories can be so compelling. They aren't just roadmaps to success, they include information about the pitfalls you might come up against too. It all makes for interesting reading, and it's not like you have to do it all at once. You can start out small by finding the time to read a couple of pages every day. Once you start getting into their stories, you'll be inspired to read some more. Before you know it, you'll have read a bunch of really good books and learned a lot. Trust me, once you get started, it won't feel like homework or studying."

I tried to look thoughtful, but I was actually thinking about my schedule. It was already really tight and I wasn't sure I'd be able to find any extra time to read. Again, I felt Granddaddy surveying me.

"Look around at your classmates and think about the amount of work they do. In one sense, you're all equal... you're all expected to do the same amount of work. All that ordinary knowledge is helping you build an ordinary foundation for your future. Some of your classmates will settle for what they get taught in the classroom and try to build their future with that. They'll do an ordinary amount of work and be satisfied with their ordinary future. If they want more... if you want more, then you have to understand that it will require more effort on your part.

"Extraordinary futures are the result of extraordinary effort. Every extra minute you utilize today is helping you build your future. You're the one who gets to decide how many extra minutes are needed. You're the one who gets to decide how extraordinary you want your life to be. Every extra minute you apply strengthens your Kaizen."

Granddaddy had stopped talking and was probably waiting for me to say something, but I still didn't have anything to say. I wasn't ready to commit to doing more work. I wanted to know what the heck a kaizen was, but Granddaddy started talking before I could ask him.

"Come to think of it, maybe one of the biggest advantages the Romans… or the Egyptians for that matter had was that they didn't have smart phones."

"What?" I asked, totally thrown off by his comment.

"I get so annoyed when people say aliens built the pyramids. It seems to me that aliens with enough technology to travel through space would have had the technology to build the pyramids much quicker. The people who lived back then were absolutely capable of building them. Their lives were very different from ours too. One of their greatest resources might have been time. They had the people, the raw materials, and no smart phones or video games. They had the time to build the pyramids."

The movie *Gladiator* popped into my mind and I chuckled at the thought of Russell Crowe dressed as a gladiator checking his text messages.

"If you were to add it all up, how much time do you think you've spent playing video games?"

I shrugged. I honestly didn't know. I'd never thought about it.

"Listen, I'm not trying to give you a hard time about

how you're spending your time. You're doing a great job. But when it comes to finding the time, the only way to find it is to believe it can be found. You won't find any time at all if you decide there aren't any extra minutes in your day before you even start looking."

"You're right. I know I can probably find a couple of minutes a day. You know Granddaddy, I really like hearing all this stuff..." I paused.

"But?" Granddaddy asked and then waited.

"But... I almost feel like I'm not doing enough now. When we started talking, I was feeling pretty good about things... I guess what I really want to ask is... will it ever be enough? I don't want that ordinary life. I want more than that, but man, I've got a pretty full schedule."

Granddaddy smiled. "Here's the thing. It doesn't matter what I think. It only matters what you think. Every journey comes with hurdles and struggles, but that doesn't mean you have to suffer through the process. And right now, it sounds a little bit like you're thinking you have to suffer by giving something up so you can keep moving forward. Think about your workouts. How do you feel at the end of a workout?"

"I feel great. Glad it's over, but stronger. I feel like I've accomplished something and I'm ready for... I don't know, for whatever."

"Exactly. It was work, hard work, but you do it anyway. You work out because you know it's going to help you. Did you feel that way after the first time you worked out?"

"Oh man, that first time just about killed me."

Granddaddy laughed. "I can believe it. I bet it took you a few weeks to get into the flow of working out too."

"Yeah, it did. But once I got going it was nothing. I had a plan and I knew what to do. It was easy really." Then I smiled at Granddaddy nodding my head. "Ohhhh, I get it."

Granddaddy nodded his head approvingly. "Exactly. Once you got started, it got easier. What matters most is how you feel about your efforts. If you find yourself suffering through the process without experiencing any kind of gain, that's when you want to stop and take a closer look at what you're doing. Don't be afraid of the work ahead of you. Focus your attention on the work in front of you. Focus on building your Kaizen."

11

The Marshmallow Test

"Good, better, best. Never let it rest. 'Til your good is better and your better is best."

- Unknown Author

This time I spoke up before Granddaddy could continue. "What the heck is a Kaizen?"

"Well, it's another secret I learned during World War II."

"Did you learn it from Colonel Reynolds?" I asked.

"I learned a lot of great lessons from Colonel Reynolds and General Eisenhower, aka Ike, while we were fighting Hitler. I learned things that kept me alive during the war, and things that helped me come home filled with knowledge, wisdom, and insight as a result. Thanks to them, and all the other great men I served with, I can proudly say I'm a part of what journalist Dan Rather called *The Greatest Generation*. We were the generation that survived the Great Depression. We won World War II and then we came home and worked on building the United States of America."

The pride in his voice came through his words, but he looked sad. "It's strange. Back then, people said the whole name... The United States of America. It was like it meant more back then. Now, people don't say it like that. Now they just say USA."

I could tell he felt bad about that. "I wish I could be a part of something like that... part of a Greatest Generation."

"You have different opportunities ahead of you. And that's a good thing. It's one thing to have everybody on the same page and working together when it comes to fighting a war. If you aren't, bad things happen. But when the fighting's done, we need to follow our own talents and dreams, and you were asking about Kaizen."

I perked up. "So what is it?"

"Well there's a bit of a story that goes along with it. Like I said, I learned a lot about life while serving in the military, but there were other military leaders I learned from that I never met or had the privilege of serving under. To tell you about Kaizen, I have to tell you about them. There's also the marshmallow test to consider," Granddaddy said and gave me an appraising look. "Are you up to it?"

"A marshmallow test? Seriously? I would hope I'd be up to a marshmallow test. How hard can it be if that's what it's called?"

"I guess we'll find out. Right now, in order for you to truly understand the secret of Kaizen, you need more background information. Let me see," Granddaddy said peering at me. "Where do I start? I guess we need to talk a little bit more about World War II.

"Initially, the United States wanted no part of what was going on in Europe. Hitler knew we were still suffering from the effects of the Great Depression and had determined it would take the United States a full two years to produce and transport a fully equipped and fully trained fighting force all the way to Europe. But Japan bombed us at Pearl Harbor. With Winston Churchill's urging, President Roosevelt finally decided to take this country to war and declared the United States an "Arsenal of Democracy" against both Hitler and Japan."

Granddaddy nodded his head like he agreed with President Roosevelt. "It was a bold move, but it left our country with a huge challenge. Roosevelt, with some help from Churchill, had decided that we needed to defeat Hitler first. Most of our resources were being dedicated to defeating Hitler anyway. But now we were sending our men to fight—in opposite directions! Hitler was probably pretty happy when he heard that. Now that the United States was going in two different directions, he figured that by the time we could get our military forces over to Europe, he would have already won the war. And he might have been right except for one thing. Any chance you might know what I'm talking about?"

I was listening to every word he was saying, but I didn't have a clue what he was talking about. I shook my head hoping he would keep going.

Granddaddy shrugged. "I had a feeling you wouldn't. But only because it isn't in a lot of history books... at least not as much as it should be. The reason we were able to pull off the impossible was because the women of this country stepped in and took over the work of the men so the men could go and fight. Our women worked in automobile factories that had been turned into war factories, 24 hours a day, 7 days a week, 365 days a year."

"Women?" I asked, surprise evident in my voice. "Really? I thought you were going to say it was some kind of secret weapon no one knew about."

Granddaddy looked at me. "Well, they were kind of a secret weapon. Hitler certainly didn't take them into account. He underestimated our resolve, and our women. Our women helped put our men in a position to be on European soil, fully equipped, fully armed, and ready to fight in less than six months while simultaneously equipping another set of troops to fight in Asia against Japan after Pearl Harbor."

"Wow! That's impressive," I said. "I never realized women played such a big role in World War II."

"Most people don't know. Again, it's not a fact that's in your history books. People also don't know how many lives were lost in war factory accidents. We lost more women in the factories than we did soldiers during the first six months of the war."

I was stunned by this information. "In all the old war movies I've ever seen, all the women do is serve coffee, dance, sing, or be nurses. I don't get it. War movies always seem to be about how brave the men are. Why didn't they show what the women were doing too? Why didn't they show it like it really was?"

"The answer is complicated. With the black and white war movies, they did it that way because people needed to keep their moral up. People didn't need to be reminded of the price they were paying for being at war. They were surrounded by it every day, so the movies were made with happy endings. They romanticized them as a way of keeping hope alive.

"As times changed, movies started showing more drama because film makers felt like the government wasn't telling the public everything that was going on. So those movies showed more about the tragedies of war. They were still focusing on the glory of the fight, and the bravery of our men, but the endings weren't always happy.

"It's only recently that we've started seeing women get recognized as soldiers in movies. It's really sad that all the women who worked tirelessly to support our victories have never really been represented or recognized for the depth of their contribution in those World War II movies—or at any other time in history."

"It doesn't seem very fair."

"You're right. It isn't fair, but that's one of the things that happens with war. Everybody pays a price. It doesn't matter which side you're on either. The men and women of every country involved with World War II did what they had to do to keep going, to keep hope alive. I'm truly grateful for all the support we got from home during those hard times. Even for those silly romantic war movies. But let's get back on track. Now where did I leave off?"

"Kaizen?" I offered hopefully.

"Not yet. We're still leading up to that... and the marshmallow test." Granddaddy smiled. "Can't forget about that."

I shook my head, but Granddaddy ignored it.

"Okay... We were at war on two fronts. The Japanese war machine did a number on us at Pearl Harbor and needed to be stopped if this country was going to survive. That job fell heavily on the shoulders of one man. With most of our country's resources battling Hitler in Europe, he was faced with the task of defeating the Japanese in Asia with only the bare minimum of soldiers and supplies. This American's name was General Douglas MacArthur, the son of the great American General Arthur MacArthur. This amazing father-son team is the only father-son team in the history of the United States to be awarded with the Medal of Honor while both were still alive. You know this Kaizen secret you're so eager to learn?"

"Yeah?" I responded with guarded enthusiasm.

"I learned Kaizen because of General Douglas MacArthur. But listen carefully... I've never met this American legend. This is just another example of the magical power of books!"

"I've never met him either," I joked. "But I do remember the name MacArthur from my history books. I'm pretty sure there wasn't anything about Kaizen though. I think I'd have remembered that."

"I'm pretty sure they didn't mention Kaizen in your history books too. Any chance you remember anything else you learned about MacArthur?"

I started wracking my brain and remembered a picture of a general with a pipe. Then I remembered something else and blurted it out. "President Truman fired MacArthur during the Korean war. Is that right?"

Granddaddy looked at me, shook his head a little, and then continued. "Yes, that's correct, but that was just a headline. Macarthur was a brilliant military leader and did a lot more than get fired by Truman. He fought in World War I, World War II, and the Korean War. In 1944, he became one of only five men in the history of the United States to rise to rank of General of the Army. MacArthur had commanded our Pacific forces against Japan, and when the war was over, he was appointed Supreme Commander of the Allied Forces in Japan."

Some of the things Granddaddy was saying started jogging my memory. "Now that you mention it, I do remember studying some of that stuff. Didn't he rule Japan?"

"Yes and no. He definitely had a tremendous effect on the country after the war. He helped Japan create a democratic constitution that's named after him and is still in use today. He broke up Japan's big companies, like Roosevelt had done with the huge companies and corporations that were starting to monopolize our economic landscape. MacArthur helped Japan start labor unions. He helped them rebuild their country and get back on track so they could compete with the rest of the World's industrial powers."

"It's really weird hearing you talk about this. I remember studying parts of it now. It's different hearing you talk about it because it sounds real now. I remember some dates too. I remember December 7th 1941. That was the day they bombed Pearl Harbor. And I remember May 8th 1945. That's the day the war was over. I remember the dates because I got tested on them. But now... I don't know... it's weird hearing you talk about people who were there. You were there."

I looked at Granddaddy but it was hard to imagine him suited up as a soldier. He was Granddaddy, but he had also been one of those men—like the ones in the pictures in my history book.

"You're right. I was there. But I'm here now, right where I want to be. I wanted to tell you about MacArthur because if it weren't for him, we probably wouldn't be talking about Kaizen at all. He didn't create it, but he was indirectly responsible for its application. Like I said, after World War II, MacArthur was put in charge of helping a war-torn Japan repair itself. But he was doing it without cell phones. There was no internet, no email. He couldn't even count on being able to complete a regular old-fashioned phone call. I bet you can't even imagine that."

I nodded. He was right about that.

"MacArthur had to work with the people around him, utilizing the resources he had. One of the things he did that was really smart was to talk Dr. William Edwards Deming in to coming to Japan to help. Deming was an American who had been raised on his Grandfather's chicken farm in Iowa. He loved math and had earned PhDs from Yale University in mathematics and physics. He was a very smart and capable man, and when these two great minds got together, that was when the concept of Kaizen started taking root. Not here in the United States of America, but in war-torn Japan."

"Did they make it up?"

"Yes and no. They didn't create the concept itself. The idea has been around for a while. Deming had been trying to get people in this country to work with the idea for years, but people weren't interested. It got the name

Kaizen in Japan."

I was trying to stay focused, but I was getting frustrated. "Is there a reason why you aren't telling me what it is? Do you think I won't understand? Can't you just tell me what Kaizen is?"

"Can I tell you about the marshmallow test first?"

"Sure.... Whatever," I sighed and turned to look at him. "Look. I'm sorry. You know I want to hear all of this. It just seems like there's a reason you aren't telling me what Kaizen is. If there's a test I have to take, can't I take it so we can be done with it and move on?"

"There's only one question."

"Ask," I said.

Granddaddy looked back at me. "If I tell you about Kaizen first, you might not understand it as well as you would if you were to hear about the marshmallow test first. Of course to hear about the marshmallow test means waiting to hear about Kaizen. So the question is, are you willing to hear about the marshmallow test first if it will help you understand Kaizen better?"

"And then you'll tell me about Kaizen after that?"

"Yes."

"Then bring on the marshmallow test."

Granddaddy rewarded my answer with a big smile. "Marshmallow tests have been around for a while now. The research started at Stanford University in the late 60's and early 70's with a group of psychologists trying to decide how old kids were when they started to develop the ability to wait for something they wanted. In other words, they wanted to know if these kids could delay gratification. The results were so interesting that other researchers focused right in on the interesting part and did their own marshmallow tests.

"They would have a kid between the ages of four and six sit at a table. On the table was a plate with one marshmallow on it. The researcher explained to the kid that they could eat the marshmallow right now, or, they could wait 15 minutes and then get another marshmallow. If they ate the marshmallow now, they'd still have to wait the 15 minutes, but they wouldn't get another marshmallow. The researcher then left the room for 15 minutes."

"Really? That's the marshmallow test?"

"I know. It sounds really simple, but this is what they found out. When they checked in on the kids who were given the test years later, the kids who had waited 15 minutes to get the extra marshmallow turned out to be more successful and appeared to be happier with their lives."

"So let me get this straight. You've been giving me a marshmallow test?" I said trying not to sound as annoyed as I was feeling.

Granddaddy shrugged. "The answer is yes. But I wasn't doing it because I wanted to know if you'd be willing to wait. I wanted *you* to be aware of the choice you made."

I stared at him.

"The marshmallow test is interesting. And maybe there is a link between success and our ability to wait for a greater reward. But I think there's more to it than that. I think anybody is capable of waiting if they have the right goal in front of them. After all, if you don't have a goal or a good reason to wait, then why bother. Why bother with the step-by-step work if the goal it's leading to isn't meaningful to you?

"Sadly, that's the way it is for a lot of people. They do the work, but they don't care about the goal because it isn't their goal—it's someone else's goal. Why work harder if there's nothing in it for them? Instead, they say "the heck with this" and move onto something else. Think about your teammates. I bet you have a few teammates who play sports just because they can. Think about your classmates. How many of them have jobs? How long do they keep them? You're the same age as they are and you have two jobs, *and* you study, *and* you work out, *and* you play two sports."

I could feel myself starting to puff up a little again.

"When it comes to the kids who ate the marshmallow, and by the way, two-thirds of them ate it, why did they eat it? What if they'd just had lunch and weren't hungry enough to be interested in waiting 15 minutes? What if they didn't really like marshmallows enough to wait 15 minutes for another one? Maybe they ate the one in front of them because they were kids. Is it okay to use a marshmallow as an indicator of future success? How would you feel if someone asked you one question and then told you your future based on one single answer?"

"I wouldn't like it."

"No one would. Especially if their one question was the wrong question. The researchers had their goal, but did it have anything to do with the kid's goal? We do our best work when we have goals that are meaningful to us. That's why goals are so important. That's why I knew you could pass the marshmallow test. You have goals. You know that sometimes you have to get through one door before you can get to the next door. Not everyone understands that. And then when they do set goals, they make the mistake of choosing goals they don't have any control over. For example, what would happen if you set a goal of winning a football game?"

"That's not a good idea," I said. "I can't decide our team is going to win a game. All I can do is prepare as best as I can and then put all my effort into everything I do. If we win, we win."

"Exactly!" Granddaddy beamed. "You can't plan for your team to win. Winning or losing is the result of the contest. The only thing you have control over is what you bring onto the field. I wish more kids had your kind of insight. But that's not really a fair thing to say either. There are plenty of kids who wonder about all these things. I bet some of your old friends think about stuff like this too."

Granddaddy shook his head. "These are the kinds of things every kid should be learning. They need guidance so they can make better choices earlier in life. That's one of the things about Kaizen. There isn't an age limit to learning it. If the United States embraced Kaizen the way they do in Japan, you'd already be applying Kaizen to your life, and so would your classmates. Don't get me wrong. It wouldn't cure everything that's upside-down for kids, but it would be a good place to start."

"So I don't have a Kaizen yet?"

"You already apply many Kaizen principles in your life. You just don't know it. Are you ready to hear the secret of Kaizen?"

"Bring it on."

12

Kaizen

"There is always space for improvement, no matter how long you've been in the business."

- Oscar De La Hoya

"The word Kaizen breaks down to Kai—which means change, and Zen—which means good. It literally means change is good, or change causes improvement. Other people say it means: self-changing for the best of all. The idea of Kaizen was already a part of the Japanese culture prior to the war. It wasn't until after the war that it became thought of as a constant and never-ending commitment to increasing the quality of Japanese businesses every single day.

"What's really interesting is that MacArthur originally brought Dr. Deming to Japan to help the Japanese prepare for their 1951 census. But because of his background in statistics and concepts of quality, Deming started lecturing to Japan's chief executives and the *Union of Japanese Scientists and Engineers* about how small improvements to the quality of a process could result in increased productivity and market share.

"This thinking helped Japan get back on its feet quicker after the War. By 1951, the Japanese thought so highly of Deming for his contributions to Japan's progress that they created an award in his name, *The Deming Prize*."

"That's cool. What do you have to do to win the prize?" I asked.

"It's awarded for contributions to the field of Total Quality Management. If you want I can give you more details," Granddaddy said with a smile.

I grimaced. "That's okay. I think I got the basics."

Granddaddy continued, "There was another interesting thing that happened as a result of Deming's influence. The US Air Force offered training to Japanese businessmen based on Deming's approach. One of the people who took part in the program was a man named Mr. Sakichi Toyoda. He was the founder of Toyota... yes, the car Toyota!"

"So Dr. Deming had something to do with Toyota too?"

"To some degree. I think the point here is that Japan had been devastated by WWII. They knew there was work to be done and they were willing to do it. What they needed was a process. Deming's ideas became embedded in their approach to rebuilding their industries, their economy, and their lives.

People became personally invested in looking at what was in front of them and making sure that whatever they were producing was the best it could be. Everybody was a part of the process too. It wasn't just management's decision. It was the people standing in front of the machines too. They all worked together, each person committed to bringing the best of themselves to their work so the combined end product would also be a reflection of their best too."

"I may not be that old, but even I know people don't do that around here. There used to be a great pizza place down the block. We went there all the time, but then they hired this new guy and it wasn't the same. He didn't last long, but even after he left the pizza wasn't as good. I don't know... maybe that's not what you were talking about."

"Oh, but it is. It's exactly what I'm talking about. Japan really embraced the concept that everybody is part of the process—even the little guy making the pizza. When they applied the idea that when everyone is a part of the process, and everyone brings their best to the job, the end result is the best product available. The result for Japan was becoming one of the most powerful economies in the world, second only to the United States. Not only that, Deming turned down all the royalties he could have earned for all the systems and products he invented while helping Japan become the top industrial power it is today."

"So that's Kaizen?" I asked a little confused.

"Yes, those are the basics of Kaizen."

"But I don't get it. I don't have a business. I don't work in a big company or anything like that. I have a couple of jobs, but they're simple jobs. I'm just a teenager. How does this relate to me?"

"Just a teenager?" Granddaddy asked. "Does that mean you aren't smart enough or old enough to start your own business? I understand how it might not sound like it has anything to do with you, but think about it for a minute. Think about the way people talk about kids your age. I hear what people say too. They think teenagers don't know how to commit to anything. They think you all give up before you try. They think you expect everybody to take care of you rather than stepping up and taking care of yourself. Is that how you see yourself?"

"No!" I shot back. "I can take care of myself. I've been doing it for years now."

Granddaddy nodded his head. "The sad part is that if the idea of Kaizen had been embraced by our country and in the way we raise our kids, you and your friends might already have a business going. The last part of the story with Dr. Deming is that when he tried to get people in the United States to employ his ideas, no one was really interested. It wasn't until the 1980s, when the United States started losing economic ground to the quality of Japanese products, that they finally started grasping the value of Deming's ideas."

Granddaddy looked at me. "You may not see a bunch of business opportunities in front of you, but that doesn't mean you can't employ Kaizen to your life right now. Like I said, you already are. Dr. Deming believed the philosophy and ethics of quality work and reducing waste would eventually give the Japanese the ability to dominate the markets of the World. He was right, but he also taught that quality was not just a matter of meeting certain standards. It was a living, breathing process of never-ending improvement."

I looked out at the rain, trying to wrap my brain around what he was saying. Granddaddy must have read the expression on my face.

"Let me repeat that last sentence again. Dr. Deming

taught that quality was not just a matter of meeting certain standards, but rather was a living, breathing process of never-ending improvement. In short, he wasn't just talking about business, he was talking about a way of life too. Can you see how that might relate to you and all your fellow teenagers?"

"Um... maybe. You're saying that I can use Kaizen in my life right now? That I don't have to be in business to use it?" I looked at him hopefully.

"Yes, that's exactly what I'm saying."

I was glad I got the answer right, but I didn't really understand what he was talking about. "I've never heard of anything like this before. It sounds like a good idea, but if it really is good, then how come I've never heard of it before."

Granddaddy sighed. "One reason is really silly and definitely sad, but it's true. We don't have an English translation for the word Kaizen. We have no word in our entire language that stresses small, continuous, never-ending improvement. People can be close minded too, and after the war they might have heard the word Kaizen, but there was very little chance of people in this country employing a concept that even remotely sounded like it had anything to do with the Japanese."

"Huh. That's the reason?"

"There are lots of reasons," Granddaddy said. "We had our own focus here. We didn't suffer the extensive structural damages they experienced in Europe and Asia, and our country had already proved it was capable of rebuilding after tough times. This was just another tough time for us, so we employed the same practices we had employed all along. We didn't feel like we needed something like Kaizen. We were all working towards the *American Dream*."

"Now that, I've heard of."

"I'm sure. That's one of the things I was fighting for when I was in Europe. We all did our part so we could come home and claim our part of the American dream. I'm curious. What do you think the American Dream is?"

I shrugged. "I don't know. Like maybe owning my own house and having my own business and being able to retire early so I can do whatever I want to?"

"That's pretty much what most people think the American Dream is. Maybe that's why so many people can't seem to achieve it."

"What do you mean?" I asked.

"Well, those are good things, but it's hard to imagine a home and a business would be everybody's idea of a happy and successful life. Maybe that's one of the big differences between the American Dream and Kaizen. With the American Dream, we're taught to invest in our long term future. With Kaizen, it's about investing in our everyday life."

I thought about that for a minute. "Doesn't Anthony Robbins say something about constant improvement?"

"He does," Granddaddy said. "He created the acronym C.A.N.I. The letters stand for *Constant and Never-ending Improvement*. Robbins believes that if there is a chance of obtaining true security in this world, then it comes from knowing that every single day you are improving your life in some way. Through CANI, you're always growing, making yourself more capable, and bringing your honest and best self to whatever you're doing. When this becomes a way of living, you become a welcome addition to your family, friends, community, and workplace. Robbins said that this commitment is the only true sense of security a human being can know."

"What does that mean... the only security you can know?"

"Well, we were just talking about the American Dream, but if you think about it, there's no guarantee everyone's going to get it. A lot of people will get there, but will they be secure when they do? Do you know what a foreclosure is?"

I nodded.

"There are plenty of people who achieved their dream of owning a home but then couldn't afford it and ended up losing it. They lost the security of having a home. I think what Robbins means is that the things we can truly feel secure about are the things we carry with us through life. When you commit to something like CANI or Kaizen, your sense of security isn't determined by the things you collect or by what goes on around you. Your true security is in knowing you are always striving to be at your best self and to bring your best self to the situation, no matter what you're doing... even if it's just making a pizza."

"I do like pizza," I said with a smile.

"There are a lot of other people who believe in this path too. Helen Keller believed security is a superstition. She said, "Life is either a daring adventure or it's nothing". She had some serious handicaps to work with and yet she didn't back down and let others do her work. She got out there anyway.

"Sometimes it's hard for people to see life like that though. They don't feel strong enough or they're just plain afraid. It's easier for them to go home, lock the doors and windows, and pull the shades tight. All they have to do is watch a little TV or read the newspaper to have their belief that home is the safest place verified."

"That's sad," I said. "First of all, it isn't always safer inside. Maybe it is compared to being outside… I'm just saying. But I get how it's like we've become prisoners, only instead of having someone lock us up, we lock ourselves up."

Granddaddy nodded. "I like to think the people in our country will come to understand there are other ways to reach for success and security. There are definitely people working on providing more opportunities for hearing about it. There are researchers, psychologists, life and success coaches, and others who have embraced the concepts of Kaizen and CANI who are always analyzing and dissecting success.

"They know success leaves clues. They know Kaizen and CANI are a part of it. They want us to know it too. We've already improved on our understanding of it by developing a new acronym—C.A.N.D.I. It stands for *Constant and Never-ending* ***Deliberate*** *Improvement*. The thought here is to stop shooting blindly for improvement. Deliberately, scientifically, and systematically pursue excellence by constantly improving on things that have already been proven to bring success."

"I like that they added the word deliberate," I said. "It gets right to the point that it doesn't just happen, we have to do it. I think that's the big problem. People are too lazy to do things."

"Some people are, but a lot of people are afraid. They don't know how to take action because nobody has ever taken the time to explain it to them. Think about it this way. You started with a book. You had coaches who recognized the potential in you and worked with you and encouraged you. Would you be where you are right now if those things hadn't happened?"

I shrugged. I didn't want to think about what my life might have been like. Would I have ended up like my brother?

Granddaddy shook his head. "I don't know the answer either. What I do know is that even with those advantages, your success is still the result of your decision to show up and do the work—even when it's not a whole lot of fun. But how great does it feel when you put your sincere and honest effort into the things you do because you've committed to a path of improvement?"

"Gotta admit. It feels really good." I turned and looked at Granddaddy completely surprised by what I had just realized. "And no one can take it away from me. Not now, not ever."

13

New Friends from the Past

"There is more treasure in books than in all the pirate's loot on Treasure Island."

- Walt Disney

I expected Granddaddy to respond to what I'd said, but he was quiet now too, almost like he was giving me time to think about it. I had to admit, it felt good—almost powerful. Not in a "go out and take on the world" kind of way. It was more like knowing that I probably really could do whatever I put my mind to. That's what I'd been doing so far. I'd just never thought of it like that before.

In sports, there's always someone trying to do the same thing you are—win. But that wasn't what I was feeling now. Right now it was more like I understood that everything I had accomplished up until now was totally because I had done the work. No one had done it for me. No one had forced me to do it. I didn't hit the snooze button on my alarm clock. I got up, and I put everything I had into the work ahead of me. Just the thought of all that

I had accomplished so far blew my mind because now, when I looked back at what I'd done, it almost looked easy.

To be honest, it really hadn't been that hard to work out. I liked it. It was easy practicing because I liked being prepared to compete. Up until this minute though, I'd thought it had been a struggle. Yes, some days were tougher than others, but for the most part it was always easy because I was doing it for a reason. It felt even better realizing I wasn't doing it just to be prepared in case I needed to defend myself against Pops. Now I was doing it because it felt good to push myself to achieve more. Now I could see how each success inspired me to push a little harder. I shook my head in disbelief.

"Why are you shaking your head?" Granddaddy asked.

I shrugged my shoulders again. "I don't know. It's weird to think about this stuff. I've never thought about myself like this... like there was anything more. I know I'm old enough for a lot of things, but I've never thought about myself as anything other than a kid in high school just doing time until I could get out on my own. The stuff you're talking about makes me wonder if I'm more than that."

"Good... because you are more than just a kid in high school. The truth is, you and all your classmates are more than that. You're all very close to being adults and going out into the world. I wish your classmates had some of the same drive and determination you have."

"But wouldn't that get in the way? If we all wanted the same things, wouldn't that be a problem?"

"If you all wanted the exact same thing it might be, but it doesn't happen like that in the real world. We all want different things because we all have different likes and dislikes."

I looked at Granddaddy. "How did you know what you wanted?"

"I didn't at first. I knew I wanted to get out of the house and I decided to enlist, but I didn't have any idea after that. It was when I started listening to Colonel Reynolds that I began to think about other things. Even then I didn't come back with a clear path in mind. I wasn't anywhere near as focused as you are."

"So how'd you do it? How'd you get where you are now?" I asked, realizing I still didn't know much about Granddaddy, what he did, or how he'd become successful.

"Friends and mentors."

I thought about that for a few seconds and then stared at the ground. I didn't really have a lot of friends, and I didn't know anyone besides Granddaddy and my coaches who said anything worth listening to.

"When I was your age," Granddaddy continued, "I didn't have a lot of friends. Not only that, I was so determined to enlist, I didn't tell anyone about my plans. I didn't trust anyone enough to talk about my ideas or dreams."

I understood that feeling.

"After the war, I had a lot of questions and no one to ask. I wasn't serving under Colonel Reynolds anymore and I didn't know what to do next. It was a hard time because I felt very much like I had started something I might never be able to finish."

"What'd you do?" I asked, totally surprised at the thought of Granddaddy being unsure of himself.

He stared out into the storm. “One day I was walking and I remembered something Colonel Reynolds had said. He told us to look at the new recruit on our right and the new recruit on our left, and then he asked us if we knew what the difference between us would be in ten years.”

Granddaddy leaned towards me conspiratorially. “I was very relieved he didn’t ask me for the answer because I didn’t have a clue what the answer was! He explained that the difference between us as the teenagers we were now, and the men we would be in ten years, would be the books we had read and the people we chose to spend our time with. Of course, like a lot of the things he said to me, it took me a while to understand and apply his words of wisdom.

“Then, one day I walked into a book store, picked up a book, and started reading. I don’t even remember what the book was. I just opened it up to the middle and started reading and it was like listening to Colonel Reynolds all over again. I was so grateful for that first book. So grateful I had remembered what Colonel Reynolds had said. When I started reading, I didn’t feel so alone anymore. I felt like I was having a conversation with someone I would have been friends with if we’d been able to meet in person.”

“You didn’t get to meet the guy who’d written the book? Did you try?”

Granddaddy chuckled. “No. That wasn’t possible. He’d been dead for a very long time.”

“You don’t remember who he was?”

“Not anymore. I’ve read so many books since then that I can’t remember who the first author was. Ever since that first book though, I’ve grown to think of each author as a friend. Each of them did one of the most meaningful things a friend can do. They cared so much about me that they shared their knowledge and wisdom for living a long, meaningful, purposeful, and happy life. They became my role models. What's even more interesting is that some of them became role models for things I decided I didn't want."

"What?"

"Well, just because someone's written a book, that doesn't mean you're going to agree with what they say. When I disagree with what they've written, I try to understand it from their point of view. In life, it isn't enough to say you disagree with what someone says. It won't carry any weight until you can explain how what you think is different from what they think. It would be like someone telling you they didn't like your wrestling technique, but couldn't tell you why, or what they think you should be doing instead."

I nodded my head.

"I never dismiss an author just because I disagree with what they said. In fact, it's when I disagree with what they've said that I'm more likely to get a deeper understanding of what I believe. So I give authors the same respect friends give each other. I respect their arguments and chalk it up to an agreement to disagree."

I chuckled. "My girlfriend… I mean Jenn, says that sometimes." I mimicked her voice as best as I could. "We'll just have to agree to disagree with this one."

Granddaddy laughed. "What do you think would happen if you didn't? If you didn't let it go and kept trying to make your point?"

"We'd probably get into a fight... unless one of us backed down."

"That's another great thing about all my author friends. They don't fight me or bully me into agreeing with them. They give me time to contemplate and think about what they've said. And, they're always ready to continue the conversation when I'm ready to read more."

I shook my head, but with a big smile on my face. "You're so cool sometimes. I've never met anyone who'd admit to having a bunch of dead friends."

"Maybe not, but they were my first role models after the war. I have a lot of living friends too, and believe it or not, they feel the same way about their book role models too. It's one thing we have in common. We understand that knowledge is a dead-end unless it's shared."

"Okay, so who's one of your favorite dead friends? Who did you learn something from that really impressed you?"

"All of them pretty much had at least one interesting thing to say, but there are a few who come to mind. First of all, I want to be clear that I'm not talking about reading text books like your history book. That's a great starting point, but I'm talking about people whose lives have been captured in words so that they can be shared with people interested in finding out more. Some stories have been chronicled by other people. Some are autobiographies. All of them have knowledge and wisdom to share. When I think back, one of the most interesting people I've ever read was about Socrates."

"We were talking about him earlier, right?"

"Yes. As I said, he was a Greek philosopher who was

always asking questions. He believed we already have all the answers inside of us. We just need to ask or hear better questions to get us looking in the right places."

"That's kind of like what you were saying about reading books and being able to explain why we agree or disagree with what they are saying?"

"Well said!" Granddaddy exclaimed, his look, one of approval. "When I read about Socrates, I understood what he meant. Don't ever let anyone stop you from asking questions. I also decided it was probably smarter to ask some of those questions inside my own head first, or to do some research before asking someone else out loud. If you remember that, you won't fear situations where you don't immediately know the answer. You will grow to welcome your questions because the more questions you ask, the more your life will expand."

"I can see how asking the wrong person might not be a good idea. You wouldn't want to ask a jailer how to pick a lock."

"That's an interesting analogy. What made you think of it?"

"Didn't Socrates go to jail?" I asked hoping I got it right.

"Socrates did get in a lot of trouble. Things were very different back then. Going against society or the rulers back then was pretty much a death sentence. Emperors and rulers saw death as the best deterrent for people who spoke out or physically rebelled against their rules. Socrates committed the crime of asking too many questions about why things were the way they were. Everybody kept expecting him to be put to death because he was doing it boldly and without fear of the consequences. The government was nervous about executing him because so many people were listening to him. Instead, they told him they'd spare his life if he would just stop asking questions. Can you guess what happened?"

I knew the answer to this one too because it had blown me away when I read it. "He drank the hemlock on purpose."

"He sure did. He said, "An unexamined life wasn't worth living". How ironic is it that Greece, famous for its democracy, tried to get Socrates to stop asking questions because they were worried more people would start asking questions too. And hey, I know this goes without saying, but remember that what Socrates did was powerful during his lifetime. It's not a good solution for someone living during our lifetime. Our job is to contribute as much as we can to life. You can't contribute anything if you're six feet underground. A better way to honor Socrates is to keep asking questions. "Know thyself" as he would say."

"I will," I said firmly.

"Want to know what I learned from my old friend Hitler?" Granddaddy asked.

I looked at Granddaddy in complete disbelief. "I can't believe that you would call Hitler an old friend!"

"I figured that might be a tough one to understand. It was tough for me to accept that he had something to teach me too... at first. But regardless of the personal impressions of him I developed during the war, despite the fact that I could never relate to his ideology or his methodology, I still learned from him."

"What could you possibly learn from him," I said trying

to wrap my brain around the fact that Granddaddy had just called Hitler a friend. “He was a butcher!”

It was the first time since we’d started talking that I was actually nervous about what he was going to say next. Hitler was a monster. Everyone knew it too. I stared at him, daring him to challenge what I’d said about Hitler.

“He taught all of us that power can corrupt the hearts and minds of the people who wield it, and that absolute power corrupts absolutely!”

I’d heard something like that before. I’d probably read it in my history book. “But everybody said that. How can you say you learned it from Hitler if everybody says it?”

Granddaddy smiled. “Sometimes it takes really big events for us to learn really big lessons. Just because millions of people learned it all together doesn’t mean it isn’t worth learning. It was a very hard lesson to learn too, but we know it now. There was another lesson in there that isn’t quite as clear until you start thinking about it.

“Change isn’t limited to the circle you draw around yourself while you pursue your dreams. It’s like those circular waves emanating from a pebble tossed in a pond. Change has the power to influence and affect other people’s lives too. What I learned from Hitler is to always consider who might be on the results end of the actions I take. When the results of change are likely to hurt or harm, or show no respect or consideration for life, it’s probably worth more thought before taking action.”

I was quiet while I thought about what Granddaddy had said. It floored me that he was able to so easily create a lesson out of Hitler, and I couldn’t help but wonder how many friends I would find in the books I was now determined to read. What would I learn?

I looked at Granddaddy. He had an air about him that commanded my respect. Not out of fear though. I genuinely respected him and what he was sharing with me. It gave me chills. I wondered if I'd be like him when I was his age. I couldn't wait for my adventure to begin and that was what this felt like—a new adventure. This day really was changing things. I decided right then and there I was going to start reading books and start talking to people.

14

When the Student is Ready, the Master Will Appear

"A student of life considers the world a classroom."
- Harvey Mackay

"It might not be fair to stop with mentioning just those two old friends. I've learned so many important lessons over the years. Jesus taught me to look within myself to find the Kingdom of Heaven. Buddha taught me about Enlightenment, Nirvana, and how to be happy with what I have instead of worrying about what I don't have. There's King Solomon, Mohammad the Prophet, and Martin Luther King Jr." Granddaddy grinned. "The list is quite a bit longer, but I'm sure you don't want to sit here while I go through it."

"It's kind of interesting. I've heard most of the names you've talked about today. I just never realized they were interesting before."

"You know who Gandhi was, right?"

I nodded my head.

"When I first started reading I came across something he said that really stuck with me. Gandhi said we should live as if we were going to die tomorrow, and learn as if we were going to live forever."

I nodded and tried to look thoughtful.

"Maybe you understand what that means, but I sure didn't when I read it. I think I understand it now. I talked earlier about being aware of the ripples we make with our actions. A lot of people will take the time to stop and try to predict the consequences of their actions so that they don't miss anything and end up accidentally causing damage. It's kind of a "look before you leap" strategy.

"Unfortunately, people can get so stuck worrying about the consequences that they never take action. That's what people are referring to when they say things like "Don't put off until tomorrow what you can do today" or "Live your life to the fullest" or "There's no time like the present". Each one of those phrases is in line with what Gandhi said. They are all reminders that even though we can live long lives, we experience our life one moment at a time. If we don't live that moment, the opportunity to live it is lost."

"That explains it better," I said. "It makes me think about keeping my eye on the ball. I mean... when you're on the football field, and you get the ball, there's already a plan in place. But you still have to look around to make sure it's going to work. If you can see it isn't, then you have to adjust the plan by figuring out what you can do to get yourself in a better position. Either way, you still have to go for it. Actually, it works pretty much the same way with wrestling too. The only difference is that wrestling is man against man and football is team against team."

"What do you think the second part means, the part about learning like you're going to live forever."

"I'm not sure about that. It sounds a little bit like doing homework for the rest of your life."

Granddaddy laughed. "I can't disagree. It does sound like that, and that's probably why most people quit learning after they get out of school. They feel like their head is full of enough knowledge for them to get the stuff they want. What do you think? Will that strategy work for you? Will your high school education or your college education be enough to get you where you want to go?"

"I'm not sure. If you'd asked me that question when we sat down, I might have said yes. But right now, I'm not sure... I like what you said about reading. Is that what you mean by learning?"

"That's part of it. Think of it like this. Say you really, really wanted to learn how to do something like sky diving, but you kept putting it off because you couldn't seem to find the time, or because it made you too nervous when you thought about taking that first step out of a plane. Every year on your birthday, you remember how much you want to learn how to jump, but each birthday passes without you doing anything about it. Then, one day, you're 76 years old—like I am today—and you realize you're never going to jump. How do think you'd feel? Oh... and don't forget... if you'd taken the time to learn it when you were 20 years old and first thought about it, you would have jumped at least 56 times by the time you were 76."

"Is that something you'd wished you'd done?" I asked.

"It's something I did."

I looked at him with amazement. "Wait.... Does that mean you jumped out of an airplane today?"

"No.... Not today. I jumped yesterday so I could be here with you today."

"Did you learn how to do it in the Army?"

"Nope. I wanted to do it, so I figured out how to make it happen."

"You've jumped 56 times?" I could feel my voice getting louder but I couldn't believe what I was hearing.

"Actually, as of yesterday, I've jumped 93 times. But don't lose track of the point here. If I'd given up on the idea of learning something new after quitting high school and enlisting, I probably wouldn't have made any jumps. If everybody settled for what they learned in school, we probably wouldn't have computers yet, or electric cars, or laser eye surgery, or CAT Scans. Our world continues to progress because people continue to pursue knowledge.

"Not only that, but because people continue to challenge themselves to learn and grow, when they hit 76 years old, they can look back at what they've accomplished and feel good about the contributions they've made. They probably won't stop there either because they'll be too excited about where the things they learn today will lead them tomorrow."

I hesitated, but then my question came out in a rush. "Do you think I'll ever do something important?"

"Absolutely," Granddaddy said without hesitation.

I smiled, but I was looking at the floor. "Like what?"

"I can't predict exactly what you're going to do. You get to make that decision. But I can tell you one thing I think you'll be really good at."

"What?" I asked; excited to hear what spectacular thing Granddaddy thought I would do.

"I think you're going to make a great coach one day."

"Oh," I said, looking back down at the floor.

"What's wrong with being a coach?" Granddaddy asked.

"Nothing... I guess... I just thought maybe you'd see me doing something more important."

"You'll do a lot of meaningful and important things. I don't have any doubt about that either. But I also believe that as you get older and start experiencing success, you'll remember what it was like being a teenager, and about the people who helped guide you. There isn't a day of my life that goes by without me thinking about Colonel Reynolds. You've already had great people in your life helping you. Your coaches, Tony Robbins, and now you're going to be reading about other people who will be coaching you with their knowledge and wisdom too. Sharing what you've learned along the way is like a rite of passage. Trust me, you'll have a burning desire to do it, and you'll be great at it."

I nodded, but it didn't sound all that exciting. I wanted him to tell me he thought I'd be an Olympic champion, or a millionaire, or something like that.

Granddaddy continued, "Have I told you that I wrestled in high school too?"

"No," I said surprised. "You never told me that."

Granddaddy nodded his head. "Yup. I wrestled for a couple of years before I enlisted. I wasn't as good as you are, but I had a couple of moves that worked pretty well. Years later, I got to spend some time with former United

States Olympic wrestling coach Jim Peckham. He was coaching a group of high school wrestlers on a few moves, and one of the kids asked if he could show him a variation he'd come up with.

"Coach Peckham said yes, even though he could have just as easily said no. He didn't know who the kid was, and truth be told, it was probably a little cocky of the kid to think he was going to show Jim Peckham something he didn't already know.

"I don't remember what I thought would happen, but I remember what did happen. He watched the kid, and when he was done, Coach Peckham smiled at the kid and said that his way was a good way to do the move. Then he laughed and said, "The day you stop learning, is the day you should hang it up". Like other things I heard when I was younger, it took a while to sink in, but I get it now. Live to learn and you'll learn to live."

Granddaddy turned and looked at me. "That's why I know you'll be a great coach. You've already shown how much you love to learn. At some point you're going to want to share what you've learned with other people. As soon as you start coaching, you're going to realize it's a two way street. They get something out of it, but you do too. When you're coaching, you're helping people reach for their dreams. Now, I don't know who you're going to coach. It might be kids; it might be your peers. Either way, I know you'll be great at it."

"You don't think it's too late for me to learn how to be a good coach?"

"Not at all. You're only 16. What would stop you from being a good coach?"

I looked down at the ground again and shrugged. "I don't know... I've read stuff that says my brain is already set in its ways, so it would be harder for me to learn stuff because I'm so old... and... maybe I'm not smart enough."

Granddaddy put his hand on my shoulder. "Let's be very clear about something here. Learning doesn't require a high I.Q. It requires interest, intention, and attention. If you aren't interested in something, it's not going to matter how smart you. But when you have an *intention* of pursuing your dreams and you start paying *attention* to what there is to learn about it, your brain will cooperate and start absorbing the information you're feeding it.

"Your brain craves information. Think about a video game you really liked. I bet you learned how to play that easily enough. Don't ever believe you aren't smart enough to learn. Insight, common sense, wisdom, and experience are just as important as lessons in a book, and that's something you'll figure out when you start reading. And plenty of those books will be written about, or by, people who weren't superstars at everything they did in school. You know who Albert Einstein was, right?"

I nodded.

"It's interesting because a lot of people believe he got bad grades in school but still became a Nobel Prize winner. He did win the prize, but he didn't do bad in school. His math and science scores were very high. What happened was that he was so into science that all his non-science grades suffered. He did so badly in his French classes that it delayed his entry into the school he wanted to go to by one year."

"Really?" I asked.

"Really. Richard Branson, the guy who built Virgin Records, Virgin Atlantic Airways, and Virgin Mobile, dropped out of high school when he was 16, but look at what he's accomplished. Abraham Lincoln was a lawyer and a president with only one year of formal schooling. The world is full of people who've succeeded without the advantages of a formal education."

Granddaddy stopped and turned to look at me. "But let's be clear, I'm not saying that dropping out of school is a good choice. The point I'm trying to make is that most people are smart enough when they're interested enough. You're no different. Chances are you might become an expert in wrestling first, but that's proof you have the ability to learn.

"If you want to be one of those people who reaches for more in life, that's even easier to do. Don't fool yourself into thinking there isn't anything else worth learning. Learn from others. Expand the knowledge they've shared with you by adding it to what you've learned from your life's experiences, and then make sure to share what you've learned with others so they have something they can expand on with their experiences."

"Kind of like a relay race, only instead of passing a baton between us, we're passing knowledge."

"Again, you nailed it. Seriously, being able to make that kind of observation of how one thing is similar to another, that's a very impressive thing to be able to do. I couldn't do that when I was your age. I can now though. Like I said, success isn't just about smarts. It's about desire and commitment too."

"I get what you're saying and I'm psyched to start

reading more about some of the people you talked about today."

"Who would you start with?"

"I'm not sure. Maybe Napoleon," I said and then continued. "I remember you saying that Napoleon and I had things in common. We both won a lot of fights to prove we could do more than people said we could. We didn't crack under the pressure we felt either. Instead, we both turned that negativity into a drive and a commitment to succeed."

"True," said Granddaddy.

He sounded impressed so I kept talking. "I like that. He's my new boy now! I already feel like we have a lot in common."

"Is he the only person?" Granddaddy asked.

"No," I hesitated, but then confessed, "but I have a tough time remembering names sometimes. There was one other guy you were telling me about. The one who lived around the same time as Jesus?"

"Cicero?" Granddaddy asked.

"Yeah. That's his name. Cicero. I'll try and remember it. Cicero."

Granddaddy gave me a questioning look. "What's the deal with names?"

"Sometimes I have a hard time remembering them. Like... I remember wrestlers when I see them, but it's easier for me to remember their moves than it is to remember their names." I paused, but didn't wait for Granddaddy to say what he was probably thinking. "I know that's not good. But I get a lot of people coming up to me at work, or where ever, and they start talking to me about sports. It's hard for me to remember all their names."

"So maybe names will be one of those things you have to work a little harder on because names are very important. Learning someone's name is a sign of respect. It lets people know they aren't invisible to you. I know you might not know what that feels like because so many people know you by name, but for the people talking to you, it won't always be the same. Think about what it might mean to a first year wrestler to have you remember their name once you become an Olympic wrestler. How will that kid feel about himself when you remember his name?"

The thought of it made me smile. It got me thinking about signing autographs too. Did I really need to know everybody's name for that? Maybe not for autographs, but Granddaddy was wrong when he said I didn't know what it was like to feel invisible. I knew exactly what it felt like to have people looking at you or through you like you didn't exist. I didn't like the thought of making someone else feel like that just because I couldn't remember their name.

Granddaddy interrupted my thoughts. "You can find lots of tricks for remembering people's names online. And here's another reason to remember people's names. Hammurabi, Ramses the Great, Charles Darwin, Alexander the Great, Julius Caesar, Elizabeth the 1st, Confucius, Sir Isaac Newton, Christopher Columbus, Benjamin Franklin, Andrew Jackson, Crazy Horse, Anne Frank, Tecumseh, Abraham Lincoln, Harriet Tubman, Albert Einstein, Rosa Parks, Sigmund Freud, Gandhi, Malcolm X, and Susan B. Anthony."

I just looked at him. "Do I have to remember all those

names?"

"When you start reading about people it will be easier than it seems right now. Look, we both know you won't actually be meeting any of the people I just named because... well... because they're all dead; so it might not seem like their names are important. But each of them was a living breathing person at one time too, and if their experience and knowledge helps us make more sense or success out of our lives, the least we can do is respect them by remembering their names. As far as remembering the names of people who are alive, that's just plain respectful. There are a lot of secrets I'm sharing with you today that might take a while to sink in, but I hope this isn't one of them. This is one you can do something about right now."

"I know Jenn will appreciate it."

"How do you know that?"

"She gets so mad at me because sometimes we'll be out somewhere and someone will start talking to me and I don't introduce her." I held my hand up to Granddaddy. "I know what you're going to say and you're right, but the reason I don't introduce them is because I can't remember their name. I don't know how to ask, and I don't want them to know I forgot. Of course my gir... Jenn gets mad because she thinks I'm not introducing her to them. I've tried to explain it, and I think she understands, but that doesn't stop her from feeling left out."

"Invisible?"

"Oh man, I hope not. You're right. I've got to get on top of this. You said there's stuff online I can learn from?"

"There's always stuff online you can learn from, and

learning ways to remember people's names is a good place for something like that. But don't get hooked on doing all your learning online. Books are good too. There's something nice about having a book in your hand. They're real. It's easier to read pages and sections more than once, and easier to go back to different sections of the book when you want to check something. You can take them with you too."

"Yeah, but books are expensive. I lost a school book last year and had to pay $25!"

"Don't you have a library card?"

"Yeah, I do, but the library?" I moaned.

"Yes, the library. I know it may not seem like the hippest place to hang out, but no one says you have to hang out there. All I'm suggesting is that all the people I mentioned, and all the people you're going to decide you want to learn more about, are in books you'll find in the library. And think about it, if you start there, it won't cost you a dime to spend time with those amazing people, their thoughts, their accomplishments, or their ideas.

"If you don't want to spend time in the library, you can probably go to the library's website first, pick the book you want to read, and have them hold it for you at the front desk. That way you can run in, check the book out, run out, and in less than a couple of minutes you'll be able to start reading about one of your new friends."

"Okay. I really do want to do this stuff. I'll do it," I said smiling at Granddaddy, suddenly remembering something I was curious about.

"What do you want to know?" He asked.

"I know you quit school to join the army, and I know

you went back to school, but I don't know what you did exactly. Did you graduate?"

Granddaddy looked thoughtful for a bit. "I did graduate... from high school and college. And I'm going to tell you something I don't always share with other people because some people think I'm bragging when I say it, but I have a few degrees."

"Really? What are they?"

"I have doctorates in both history and political science."

"Wow. I figured you were really smart."

Granddaddy shook his head. "That's one of the reasons I don't always tell people. They hear about my degrees and then they automatically think I'm smarter than them and that my education puts me above them. It doesn't. All it means is that I wanted to learn more. I wanted the challenge of learning and that's what school does sometimes. It challenges us to push the limits of what we know and understand."

I knew I had that confused look on my face again, but I couldn't help it.

"You actually understand this and I'll prove it to you. Remember how we talked about learning all the names and dates and stuff so you can pass a test?"

I nodded.

"Well the difference I'm talking about is when you know the names and dates, but you also understand how the story fits in there too. So when I got my degrees, I wasn't just learning more names and dates. I was learning how everything fit together. For example, obviously, I love history. But once I started learning by looking at all the information that was available, it was even more amazing. It was like I was there when they were devising strategies and making plans.

"The subjects you choose to dive into might be different for you. You might really like studying athletes. They're amazing to read about too and when you're able to connect the story with the person, their accomplishments become real and tangible things. The point is, the only thing my degrees are evidence of is the fact that I was committed and inspired to learn more about how the world got to where it is today. History didn't make me smarter than anyone else. But when I gave myself permission to learn from it, it taught me how to live today."

15

Give Yourself Permission!

"I am determined to be cheerful and happy in whatever situation I may find myself. For I have learned that the greater part of our misery or unhappiness is determined not by our circumstance, but by our disposition."

Martha Washington 1731-1802
First Lady of the United States

I wondered if I'd heard him right. "So you gave yourself permission to learn?"

"Sure did," Granddaddy replied.

"I don't get it. How can you give yourself permission to do something? Don't you just do it, or don't do it?"

"People either do something or don't do something, that's true, but giving yourself *permission* to do something or to not do something can change your whole experience."

"That doesn't make sense," I said shaking my head.

"Sure it does. Have you ever gone to a movie you weren't the least bit interested in seeing?" Granddaddy asked.

I rolled my eyes. "Chick flicks. Jenn loves them, but she doesn't want to go see them with her girlfriends. She always wants me to go with her."

"I hear you. I've been to my share of chic flicks too," Granddaddy said shaking his head. "But let me ask you this. What do you think would happen if you gave yourself permission to find something about the whole experience you could enjoy? Like giving yourself permission to enjoy spending this time with Jenn without having to think up things to talk about? Or giving yourself permission to see how happy it makes her when you take her to a movie she really wants to see."

"I've never thought of doing it like that."

"Give it a try. I can pretty much guarantee it will change your experience when you do," Granddaddy said. "Very few things in life are 100% fun, even when you're really passionate about the goals they lead to. A while back you said you really liked working out, but there must be something you don't like to do. What is it?"

"Squats…. Ugh."

"The next time you're working out and you have to do squats, try giving yourself permission to not love doing it, but also make sure to remind yourself that by choosing to do it anyway, even one of your least favorite things to do is helping you achieve your dreams."

Granddaddy turned to face me. "Sitting around and waiting for the world to give you permission to be more than you are is a waste of time. Think about it. If everyone is waiting for someone else to take charge and give them permission to be motivated, then who's left to take charge?"

"No one," I understood.

"That's right. No one. But that's what happens most of the time. People look everywhere else for permission to believe in their dreams, and when they don't get it, they give up. Even if they do get started, the next worst thing usually happens. They accomplish something and then they look at the people around them hoping for approval and recognition. If they don't get it, they give up because this time they're waiting for someone else to give them permission to enjoy their accomplishment. Either way, they're right back where they started."

"I think I understand what you're saying. There's a guy on my wrestling team… he's ranked second right behind me. But he's never happy when he wins. I think it's because his dad is always giving him a hard time. He gives him dirty looks when he loses and barely smiles when he wins. I've congratulated him before, but all he does is shrug his shoulders. He doesn't smile either. Do you think it's because he hasn't given himself permission to enjoy his wins?"

"It sounds like it. There's probably other stuff going on there too. But I'd be willing to bet that if it had started differently, if he had felt like his dad was happy with his progress from the beginning, he'd probably have been able to give himself permission to enjoy his wins too."

"That's a pretty cool way to look at it. I'm going to try that the next time I take Jenn to the movies. If I can figure out a movie she wants to see, I might even ask her if she wants to go before she brings it up. I bet that would make her really happy."

Granddaddy looked at me. “You’re smiling.”

“Sure. I feel good. Why shouldn’t I smile?”

“Just wanted to bring it to your attention. A minute ago you were rolling your eyes thinking about chick flicks, but as soon as you gave yourself permission to find some aspect of it you could feel good about, you came up with a win-win scenario for both you and Jenn.”

“Huh. So whenever I have to do something I don’t want to do—“

“Or can’t do something you want to do—“ Granddaddy added.

“I just have to give myself permission to find something about the situation I can feel good about?”

“Yup,” Granddaddy said. “And as you begin to notice how many people around you don’t know how to do this, my prediction is that you’re going to start giving the people around you permission too.”

“But I thought you were saying that other people can’t give us permission.”

“You’re right, they can’t. But when someone acknowledges our efforts, it can be enough to get us moving in the right direction. One of the reasons people don’t do this is because no one ever told them it was an option. That’s why I think you’ll be a great coach. You’ll see people succeed, but when you tell them what a good job they’re doing, you’ll make sure they realize that their accomplishments were the result of the work they put in. They aren’t the result of a coach saying it, or because they earned a check mark in the “win” column. You’ll be encouraging them and giving them permission to acknowledge the effects their efforts have had on their success."

"I think I can do that."

"I think you can too. And that's one of the skills that will make you a good leader."

"You think I'll be a good leader?"

"It's part of your plan."

"Yeah, but... you know... I hadn't really thought it through yet... like how I would do it."

Granddaddy raised his eyebrows. "You may not have planned out all the A-B-Cs of what kind of leader you want to be, but believe me, you already possess a lot of the skills. And don't get stuck on the idea that all leaders have titles. There are plenty of great leaders in this world whose only titles are Mom or Dad. Good leaders inspire the people around them to believe in themselves and their abilities. They give credit where credit is due, encourage when times are tough, and are happy to celebrate victories regardless of how big or small they are."

I smiled. "Then you must be a good leader because talking to you makes me feel like I can do just about anything."

"Why would you think you couldn't?" Granddaddy asked.

"I guess because it seems like there aren't many people who ever get what they really want." I looked at Granddaddy. "I think you did, but I don't think Pops did. I don't know if Mom did, but it's hard to believe she wanted what she's got. I don't know what my brother wanted either, but I don't think it was jail."

"It sounds a little bit like you still have doubts about your plan."

"It's more like I know where I want to go, but I also know that people shoot for things all the time and miss. I work harder because I don't want to miss." I looked down at the ground. "But what if I fail?"

"That's a good question, and I'm glad you had the courage to ask it out loud." Granddaddy paused for a minute before continuing. "Things do happen, and they aren't always good. But what you're really talking about is fear of the unknown and that's something I know a lot about. When we were fighting Hitler, we always had a plan before we made a move, but there were never any guarantees we would be successful. All we could do was commit to bringing our best to the action. It was interesting thinking about it that way too, because it got us very focused, similar to the way you get focused with your sports."

"Uh… I think your situation was a little more important than mine."

"From a historical perspective maybe, but from an individual perspective, it really isn't much different. We make plans we believe will help us accomplish our goal, but the possibility of failure is always there. The question is, which would you rather do—bring your best to the plan and face it head-on regardless of the outcome? Or, plan to bring your best but then let your fears and doubts interfere with your ability to bring your best?"

"I'd rather bring my best."

"That's what Colonel Reynolds taught me to do. When he talked to us about what was going to happen next, he never wasted one breath trying to convince us everything would be okay. Instead, he reminded us of how capable and accomplished we were. He reminded us that we were strong and capable as individuals, as a group, and in our belief of what we were fighting for. That's what we took into battle with us.

"I know that may sound more important than stepping out onto a wrestling mat, but don't kid yourself. Every time we step up to a challenge, failure is always an option regardless of how big or small, important or unimportant the challenge may seem. Do you know who Vince Lombardi was?"

"Sure. Coach of the Green Bay Packers."

"Right. Well he said it doesn't matter how many times you get knocked down, what matters is how many times you get back up. He understood that the difference between winning and losing wasn't always about actually winning the contest. Take wrestling for example. You expend a lot of energy and effort when you're out there wrestling, but think back to when you first started. Think about those early practices and matches and remember what it felt like. Did you feel like you were fighting for your life out there? Do you remember feeling like you'd gotten hit by a Mack truck after a match regardless of whether you'd lost or won?"

"It makes my body ache thinking about it," I said wincing.

"Do you remember what it felt like when you started getting tired during a match and how it felt like your lungs were on fire and about to burst while you're trying to keep up with your opponent? You had to keep going, but the more tired you got, the harder it was to feel like you could see it through. And then a thought zaps into your head—

what if I can't do this? Do I have what it takes to win?" Granddaddy shook his head. "I don't know about you, but I remember it."

"I know what you're talking about. It happened to me a couple of times in the beginning. I panicked because I realized it wasn't going well and I started thinking about losing. I didn't want to lose, but then it was like I was frozen and I had a hard time getting my body to cooperate."

"What happened?" Granddaddy asked.

"I lost."

"And then how did you feel?"

"Well, I felt like crawling off into a corner. I don't know… I guess I felt like I'd failed. I really wanted to win. But I didn't."

"So why didn't you quit?"

16

Got Excuses?

"People who are unable to motivate themselves must be content with mediocrity, no matter how impressive their other talents."

- Andrew Carnegie

I stared at him. "Why would I quit?"

"Because you didn't win."

"Yeah, but I'd been working really hard. I wasn't going to quit because I didn't win one match. I just kept trying to get better... and I did."

Granddaddy nodded his head. "And I think that's what Lombardi was talking about. What we do when we get really tired and feel like we've reached our limit. Sometimes it's easier to give up than it is to keep going and lose. Sometimes it's easier to stay down than it is to risk losing the dream."

I frowned and nodded. "I know what you're talking about."

"How so?" Granddaddy asked.

"I've been there. But after losing a few times I decided I was going to do what I had to do to win."

"And what did you decide you had to do?"

"Obviously I had to work harder to get stronger. I started paying more attention to what other wrestlers were doing, looking for things I could take advantage of. Stuff like that. But mostly I decided to win. As soon as I made that decision, I started to win."

Granddaddy chuckled.

"Why are you laughing?" I asked feeling offended.

Granddaddy shrugged. "Because I'm always amazed when people say they just decided to *win*, or to *be the best*, or *number one*, and then when they finally get there, they think it's because they made a decision to do it."

"What's wrong with deciding to be the best?"

"Nothing... nothing at all. Making the decision to be the best is an admiral quest. It's just a tough goal because you don't really have any control when it comes down to winning or losing."

"What do you mean? I'm the #1 wrestler on my team and I got there because I decided I wanted it."

"No. You got to #1 because you did the work that put you in a position to challenge for the #1 spot. The fact that you won doesn't have anything to do with your ability to choose to win."

I shook my head. "You aren't making any sense. I decided I had to win, I did what I had to do to win, and I won."

"Okay, but what would have happened if you'd done all your preparation, done your very best on the mat, and still lost. What would have happened then?"

"But that's not what happened. I won."

"I get that. But what would have happened if you'd lost."

I didn't understand what Granddaddy wanted me to say. Did he want me to say I wasn't as good as I thought I was? Well that wasn't going to happen because I knew I was good—very good. And as long as I kept working hard, I knew I was going to keep getting better. I tossed my hands in the air. "I don't know what you want me to say."

Granddaddy shrugged. "All I'm saying is that it's easy to put your talent and skill to the test when you're winning, but don't let winning become the prize you use as motivation to keep going. The fact is, you don't have any control over who's going to win."

"Sure I do. That's how I win, by taking control on the mat."

"Okay. So let's agree to disagree right now. And don't change what you've been doing because it's working. Absolutely keep deciding to win. Just think about what I said and understand that there are a lot of ways to win a contest that can't be measured by the weight of the trophy you hold up at the end."

It was my turn to laugh.

"Why are you laughing?" Granddaddy laughed.

I shook my head. "Because sometimes the things you say sound like something you'd find in a fortune cookie."

Granddaddy nodded and laughed too. "You're right. Sometimes they do... But that doesn't mean they aren't important."

"Is that why you're harping on my decision to win?"

"Not at all. But once again, I have to remind you that

you're an exception. Most people don't win. They start out the same way you did, by making an effort and putting their talent, skill, and goals to the test... and not just with sports. But if they don't win, they start being afraid to put themselves out there and really try to reach for something meaningful. Their losses hit them hard and then they give up. They don't dare risk their dreams by trying to achieve them because if they fail, and lose their dream in the process, they'll feel like they've lost everything."

"That's so sad. All they have to do is keep working. But I've seen it on the wrestling team too. Guys try out and they have some talent and do the work, but then they lose a couple of times and quit. I've never understood that. It's like they quit without ever really trying."

"Maybe it's because they've been led to believe winning is the most important part of the contest—the only thing that matters. People who believe that usually decide it's safer not to try to win than it is to risk it all and lose."

"I thought about that too in the beginning. After losing those first few matches, I felt whipped in every way. I could barely move. My head felt like it weighed 100 pounds and my muscles felt like rubber. Come to think of it, I still feel like that sometimes, but I don't think about it the same way anymore. I just accept it as part of the process."

"Maybe so, but you did something not everyone knows how to do. Instead of giving in to the pain and discomfort wrestling forces you to endure by quitting, you made the choice to deal with it and still continued to do more."

"You have to do more if you want to succeed. The more I do, the better my overall results are. It's kind of a no-brainer."

Granddaddy smiled. "I agree. But people don't learn to think like that. When they don't get the results they want, they start thinking it's because the other guy had something they don't. A lot of coaches say things like "That's okay. We'll get them next time" or "Good effort," but those kinds of words don't help.

"The fact is, losses are tough subjects and people don't know how to talk about them. It's easier to chalk it up to things like shifts in momentum, a lucky break, the crowd was on the other team's side, or they had the "home team" advantage. Those things sound good, but you can't compete against those kinds of excuses. You can't succeed if you start looking at your results and decide they were caused by things you have no control over. And this doesn't just apply to sports."

"What do you mean?" I asked.

"How about this situation? How many times have you heard kids in school complain about getting a bad grade on a test?"

"All the time," I answered.

"Kids will complain about a bad grade and come up with all kinds of excuses to explain it. The teacher was unfair, there were questions on the test we hadn't been covered in class, or the questions were trick questions."

"You missed a few," I said laughing. "The teacher didn't review the material. They weren't given enough time to study, or because of sports or work, or the test was too hard."

"So it sounds like it's pretty easy to avoid the real reason for a bad grade if all those other excuses are available."

"I guess so." I shrugged. "I know what you're getting at here. You're trying to get me to see that if I want to get better grades I have to work harder instead of coming up with excuses like the ones we just came up with."

"I wasn't talking about you. I brought it up as an example of how easy it is to look at results and blame other people and situations for them. That's what people have learned to do. Your teachers will remind you that studying will result in better grades, but they always say that."

"It's like a broken record," I said rolling my eyes.

"So why don't kids take their teacher's advice and study harder?"

"Because teachers care about grades. Some teachers are nicer than others, and it's easier to learn in some classes, but I'm not sure they really care about what we learn. I know they care about how good our grades are. If we do really bad, they look bad, so they get on our cases about studying."

"So that means if you get a bad grade it's their fault because..."

"Because they shouldn't harass us about studying. Maybe they shouldn't always blame us if we get a bad grade. Maybe if they treated us differently..."

Granddaddy continued my thought for me. "You'd get better grades?"

I shrugged. "Maybe."

"But if you could get better grades without them asking

you to study, or if they treated you differently, doesn't that mean you could get better grades anyway?"

I didn't want to answer because once again Granddaddy was right.

"That's okay, you don't have to answer. I can tell by your expression that you get it. You know your grades aren't the result of a teacher trying to get you to study. The decision to study always was, always is, always will be a choice you get to make. The challenge is looking at the situation and deciding where you want to put your energy. Do you want to invest it in studying, or do you want to invest it in rebelling against a teacher?

"You can even take it one step further and think about the results you'll get with both situations. Which result would you feel better about? A better grade that's the result of your effort, or a bad grade that gives you the opportunity to put the blame on someone else?"

I looked at Granddaddy. "Don't you think you're pushing it a little bit here? I don't think like that."

Granddaddy shrugged. "Maybe not. But I wanted to give you a really good example of a situation where people give up their own power to succeed simply because they've learned it's easier to blame other people for their failure than it is to step up and take control of their own results."

"Do you think everybody can get good grades?"

"I don't know if everybody can get better grades. I know there's a difference between setting a goal and making an effort to accomplish it, and being either too scared or too lazy to try. And those are the two extremes people get stuck between. Teachers, coaches, and mentors can give their students advice, just like bosses can tell their employees how to do something. But it always comes down to the choices we make when we're deciding how to respond."

Granddaddy sighed. "People waste so much time blaming the world for their situations. They wish things were different, but the answer is always right there in front of them."

I suddenly wondered if Granddaddy was about to expose one great big secret that would be the answer to everything we were talking about today. "What answer?" I asked totally hoping to be blown away.

"GOYA."

17

GOYA

"It doesn't matter how many times you fail. It doesn't matter how many times you almost get it right. No one is going to know or care about your failures, and neither should you. All you have to do is learn from them and those around you. All that matters in business is that you get it right once."

Mark Cuban, Entrepreneur, Author, and
Owner of the NBA's Dallas Mavericks

"What?"

"GOYA," Granddaddy repeated. "Get off your ass."

I turned away from him and started laughing.

"You think that's funny?" He asked.

"You said ass," I said laughing.

Granddaddy started laughing too. "You're right. I did. But I said a little bit more than that. Have you ever heard of GOYA before?"

I shook my head no.

Granddaddy was still smiling, but he looked out into

the rain. "I'm not surprised," he said, sounding discouraged. "Ideas like GOYA could make such a difference if people heard about them... if they understood them."

Even though it didn't sound like the one big secret I was hoping for, Granddaddy hadn't let me down yet today. "So how does GOYA work?"

Granddaddy raised his eyebrows. "I would have thought you knew exactly how it worked."

"Well... sure. I know what it means. It means getting off your ass." I tried to sound serious, but I started laughing again.

Granddaddy smiled, but he didn't laugh this time. Instead, he turned, looked at me and asked, "But how do you get started? In one way it seems like getting up and doing something would be the easiest thing in the world to do. But it can be a real challenge coming up with a meaningful reason to GOYA and do something."

"I think I have a meaningful reason," I said. At least I wanted to believe I did.

"What is it?"

I opened my mouth, but then stopped. My original reason was to stop Pops, but it turned out I hadn't needed to protect myself. So why was I still doing what I was doing? All of a sudden I wasn't so sure. I kept going because sports gave me something to do that I was good at, and was getting better at. But I didn't know if that was a meaningful reason for doing something. I looked at Granddaddy and shrugged.

"I thought I had meaningful reasons," I said. "But now I don't know if they're *meaningful*. They're definitely reasons why I do things, but are they *meaningful*? That word makes me think that maybe my reasons aren't deep enough. Like… is getting a trophy meaningful?" I looked at Granddaddy and then looked away. "Now I'm thinking my reasons might not be good reasons."

Granddaddy smiled and clapped a hand on my shoulder. "And now you know how easy it is for people to end up feeling like their dreams and goals aren't worth pursuing. All it took was one question from me to get you to question whether or not your reasons are meaningful."

That shook me right down to the soles of my feet. I didn't think anybody could get me to second guess myself, but he was right. He'd done it with one question. "But how do I know if my reasons are good enough reasons… like you said… if they're meaningful?"

Granddaddy looked thoughtful. "That's a very good question, but it's a tough one too because it isn't up to me to decide. Only you can decide if your reasons are meaningful. That's one of the reasons people struggle with applying GOYA to their lives. They look to their family and friends and hope to hear things like, 'Yes. Your reasons are meaningful. Go for it!' But that's not what they hear. Look at your situation. How many people have you told your reasons to?"

I shook my head. "I've never talked about it with anyone before today." I stared down at the floor. "Not even Jenn," I whispered.

"I totally understand. When I was your age I didn't have as much drive as you have, but I didn't tell anyone what I was doing either. I joined the army for one reason—to get away from my dad. After I'd enlisted, I had a new reason to take action—to protect our country. But when that was done, I struggled with what to do next. There were plenty of people telling me what I should do, but nothing felt right—or good—on the inside."

"What'd you do?"

"I did what most people do when that happens... I sat around with a bunch of guys in the same situation and complained right along with them."

"Really?" I was having a hard time imagining Granddaddy being like that.

"Sure. It was easy to sit and complain about how hard things were, how much I hated my job, how tight money was, how tired I was, and how no one really appreciated me. They all nodded their heads and agreed with me, and I did the same when they complained about their lives. But then one day I was listening to this older guy complaining, just like we always did, and I got mad. Not at him exactly, I was just tired of hearing him say the same things day after day and almost told him that if he didn't like the way things were then he should get off his ass and do something about it."

Granddaddy looked thoughtful. "I distinctly remember opening my mouth and closing it and looking at him, and it was like I was staring at myself only I was 30 years older." Granddaddy looked down at the ground. "It scared the crap out of me."

"Wow. That's crazy," I said.

"Tell me about it. But suddenly I had a reason. I didn't want to end up like that guy. I knew I wanted more, and right then and there, I realized that if I wanted a better life, it was up to me. It was sad too, because I also realized that if I kept hanging around with those guys, they'd be able to drag me right back to where they were.

"I liked them. They were good guys, and deciding to stop hanging out with them was definitely one of the hardest parts. I still thought of them as my friends, but I understood that we were going in different directions now. I could have tried to get them to join me, but people aren't like that. I'd found a new reason to make an effort, but they'd given up looking for a better reason to take action a long time ago."

"Wow." That was all I could say. It was so strange to hear that Granddaddy hadn't started out like he was now. He'd struggled when he was young too, and I wondered what he was like back then. Was he like his dad? Or had he been like Pops was now?

"Hey," Granddaddy said interrupting my thoughts. "I didn't tell you that so you'd feel sorry for me. I told you because it's important to understand that the reasons people do what they do are personal. There isn't one good or perfect reason. There's only the reason that motivates *you* to move in a better direction."

"So what'd you do?"

Granddaddy rubbed his chin. "That's a long story for another day. Right now it's almost time for you to go to work and there are a couple more things we have to cover before we're done."

"Okay," I said, but I was disappointed because I really wanted to hear more about what Granddaddy had done in his life.

"There's one more thing I want you to know about the time I spent with those guys back then, and it's going to sound strange, but we were happy." Granddaddy shook his head and chuckled. "Sometimes it's easy to look at a group of people and think that they have to be unhappy because of where they are and how they're living, but that's a mistake. People can be rich and unhappy, or poor and happy. I didn't have any money back then, didn't really have any ambition, but we had a good time all the same.

"I think the difference between me and the guys I was hanging out with was simply that I hadn't given up yet. I'd had some experience with success and it had made an impression on me. I wanted to be successful. I liked the feeling of it. I wasn't exactly sure what I wanted to succeed at yet, but I really believed it would make me happy, so I'd found my reason to start pursuing happiness elsewhere."

Granddaddy turned to me. "People get to decide what makes them happy. You get to decide what makes you happy. The same goes with what you choose to do. You get to decide what feels right, or meaningful, or purposeful. No one else can give you those things. No one else can tell you *what* to do to feel them either—because it's not *what* you do that matters. Let me rephrase that last part. What you do in life can matter a great deal to other people, but what's going to matter to you is how you feel when you do it. When you feel like the things you're doing are making a contribution to some aspect of life, then even the smallest contribution can be meaningful."

I was trying to follow what he was saying, but I was getting a little lost. "It doesn't matter what I do? How can that be?"

"If *what* we did was the source of our happiness, then it wouldn't matter what we did. We'd all be happy regardless of what we were doing. People make that mistake a lot. They think that doing bigger things, like owning their own company, will make them happier. It just isn't true."

"But I want to own my own company someday too. What's wrong with that?" I asked a little defensively.

"Nothing," Granddaddy replied. "It's a good goal, but owning your own company is no guarantee of happiness. Happiness isn't the result of *what* you do. It's the result of *how* you do it."

"Huh?"

"What you do will never be as meaningful, or memorable, or as motivating as how you do it. Look at it like this. Over the past couple of years you've started collecting trophies. When you look at them, what do you think about?"

I shrugged. "I don't know... maybe that it was cool that I won."

"Fair enough. Now think about all those athletes you've heard about who took illegal steroids. Do you think they feel the same thing as you do when they look at their trophies?"

"I doubt it. They cheated. They may have the trophy, but they didn't win it fair and square. If I were them, I wouldn't be able to look at them."

"So you think something different when you look at your trophies."

"I guess so. At least I didn't cheat. I worked really hard to get them."

"How do you feel about all the extra work you did in the gym? I know it was hard, I know you hate squats, and I know you don't get a trophy every time you compete regardless of how many extra squats you did. So why do you keep doing it?"

"I don't know. It may sound weird, but I like the work. I like the physical part of it and I like the challenge when I step on the mat. I know I don't win every time, but when I do win, I like the trophy too."

"It sounds like wrestling is hard work. I know why you started doing it, but now that you know you can take care of yourself, why do you keep doing it?"

I hesitated but then answered. "This is going to sound even weirder, but I'm kind of addicted to it. If I go too many days without working out, I feel like a slug. Jenn says I get grouchy when I don't work out. As soon as I work out, I feel great again."

"Well, maybe that's what happens when people get used to doing what they're doing. It's such a habit, that it becomes more like an addiction. I think that's what happened to the guys I hung out with after the army. They were so used to complaining day after day, that they couldn't go a day without complaining. They kept complaining because they couldn't come up with a good enough reason not to."

"They weren't motivated," I said.

"What do you mean?" Granddaddy asked.

"Um... If I wasn't getting the results I wanted, I'd try and figure out what else I could do to improve my results. That's how I started winning wrestling matches. I figured out what I needed to do to improve. I'd work on it to get better. It worked too. I started winning more. If your old buddies weren't interested in doing more, then either they were happy right where they were, or they weren't motivated enough to try something new." I frowned. "So instead of doing something new, they just kept doing what they always did."

"Exactly!" Granddaddy exclaimed. "Einstein nailed this situation right on the head when he said, "We cannot solve our problems with the same thinking we used when we created them." These days people call that the definition of insanity."

"Doing the same thing over and over again and expecting a different result," I interrupted.

"Yup. Thinking outside the box is another phrase people use too, but they all boil down to the same thing. If you want something beyond what you have right now, then you have to open your mind to new ideas—like reading. If you don't, you'll spend your life rearranging what you already know. As soon as you start looking outside of yourself, you'll begin to see how many things are possible. You might even discover a path you'll love every step of."

"You're talking about comfort zones. I know what those are. Comfort zones are for losers."

18

When You Help Others, You Help Yourself!

"There is no exercise better for the heart than reaching down and lifting people up."

- John Holmes

"That sounds a little harsh," Granddaddy said.

I shook my head. "I disagree. One of my coaches talked to the team about losing one day. We'd lost a few matches in a row and he wasn't happy. We thought he was going to yell at us, but he didn't. Instead, he talked about how comfortable couches can be, and how when we sit there watching TV or playing video games, the distance between us and our dreams keeps growing. After a while, our dreams start to feel like they're a million miles away and it's easier to put them out of our mind than it is to figure out how to get started.

"Then he asked us to think about people we know who spent most of their free time sitting on the couch doing nothing but watching TV or playing video games. He told us to imagine what they might look like in 20 years. Or what we might look like in 20 years if we decided to sit down and join them. It was a pretty scary thought. All I could see was Pops drinking a beer and yelling at the some sports team on TV."

Granddaddy nodded his head. "It's a good analogy, but I bet there were still people who didn't respond."

"A couple," I said.

"Some people are too scared to make a move. It's probably the saddest thing to have happen too, but it happens all the same. Momentum helps, and that's one thing winning does accomplish. It helps build momentum. You do some work, you get some good results, your confidence builds, you keep working, you win more, etc. It's easier to keep momentum going with sports though."

Granddaddy smiled at me. "There are a lot more trophies in sports than there are in life. That's why reasons are so important. If you don't have good reasons for pursuing your goals, it's very hard to stay motivated long enough to see them through."

"I get that, but why don't people do something? Why don't they just get off their... ah... butts and do something?"

"If it was that simple, they probably would. But they'd have to believe there was something better out there, and a lot of people have let that ship sail. Or they've decided they're too old, or too dumb, or that it will take too much work, or that there's no one to step in and help them, or whatever. Some people don't think they deserve anything better. But sometimes it's simply because they're too afraid to step outside their comfort zone—even when their comfort zone is in a bad place.

"It's like trying to believe the world is round when everyone around you is still convinced it's flat. You believe the world is round, you believe the people around you are wrong, but look at the risk you're taking if you start walking. You're walking away from everything and everyone you know towards something completely unknown and foreign to you. And most of the time you're walking alone. It takes a lot of faith and inner strength to start walking down that path."

"I hadn't thought about it like that before. So… how do you convince unmotivated or scared people to do something?" I asked.

"*You* can't. People have to make that decision on their own. And it's not like they can't survive if they don't make the decision to reach for something better. In this country we take care of people who are struggling. It's sad, but there are people who take advantage of those services, blaming everybody else for their problems. After a while, that becomes their comfort zone."

"But that's wrong. You can't go around blaming other people for your situation."

Granddaddy shrugged. "It's risky business to blame people for the situation they're in too. You might be right, but you don't know their situations or their circumstances. It's just as easy to blame people from a distance for their problems as it is for them to blame you from a distance for not doing anything to help them. It sets up a lose-lose situation where nothing ever changes."

"I don't get it. Then what's the answer?"

"The best answer is always to take action. G-O-Y-A and do something—anything!"

"But people don't," I said. "I see that. Heck, sometimes I don't do anything."

"Me too. Sometimes I don't do anything either."

I stared at him in disbelief. "You get stuck too?"

"Sure," Granddaddy replied. "I'm human. Back when I was really stuck I came up with a good reason to take action. But it's impossible to stay motivated all the time. There are times when you need a break. The real trick is not letting that break last too long. The longer it lasts, the harder it is to get back into the groove. Take your workouts for example. If you didn't work out for a month, what would happen?"

I thought about it. "It would hurt. I'd have lost a lot of ground in a month and wouldn't be very competitive at that point. I'd probably lose matches until I was back in shape." I looked at Granddaddy. "It would suck."

Granddaddy nodded his head. "It sure would. That's why it's important to have things you can do that keep you moving even if you aren't motivated to work on your own stuff at the moment. And, there's one sure fire action that will keep you moving. It's just as inspiring as working on your own stuff... maybe even more inspiring when you get right down to it."

"What is it?"

"Do something for somebody else."

"You mean like charity?"

Granddaddy shrugged. "Yes, that works, but there are lots of things you can do for other people that don't fall under the heading of charity. Do something nice for someone out of the blue. Like when you talked about taking Jenn to a chick flick without her having to ask. The point is to think about what you can do to help someone. Don't think money or charity, think about what someone else might need."

"I don't really know anyone who needs anything... well, I know people who might need things, but they are things I can't help with. I can't help someone get a car."

"Maybe not a car, but you know a lot about working out. Is there anybody you can think of who could use some help with that?"

"Maybe, but why would they listen to me?"

"They might not. It kind of depends on how you offer. It might not work if you walk up to someone and tell them they're doing it all wrong. Just put yourself in their shoes and remember how it felt when you first started out. When you see someone getting something wrong, think of what you would have been okay hearing back when you were making those same mistakes. The best rule of thumb is to remember that it's not *what* you say that matters as much as *how* you say it. Don't talk down to people. Don't be condescending, or rude, or mean."

Granddaddy held up his hands. "I know you won't be any of those things, but sometimes it takes a little practice to figure out how to teach or tell other people things. As long as your goal is always to treat them with the respect and dignity every human being has a right to, you'll do okay."

"What happens if they don't want any help?"

"Then they aren't ready. If that happens, your big challenge will be not taking it personally. If people aren't ready to accept what someone else is offering them, then they aren't ready. There's nothing you can do about that. You can't make someone ready to accept what you have to offer. But as soon as you realize they aren't ready, you'll find your own motivation in full force because you are ready."

Granddaddy turned towards me shaking his head. "I gotta warn you though. Doing things for other people gets addicting too. There's nothing quite like seeing a genuine smile on someone's face and knowing you played a part in putting it there. It will fill you up. And when you feel like crap, or when you're stuck, or when you can't figure out what to do next, doing something for someone else will start kicking off the cobwebs until you're ready to get back on track. It's the whole GOYA thing. When you can't GOYA for yourself, then GOYA for someone else!"

I smiled. I liked the way that sounded. GOYA... I was definitely going to have to write that down. Maybe even write it in big letters on a single sheet of paper and tape it to my wall. Maybe the inside of my locker too. GOYA... got it!

"Hey. It's stopped raining," Granddaddy said.

I looked out and he was right. The wind had died down and there was blue sky off in the distance.

Granddaddy continued, "I guess we're lucky it stopped raining before you had to take off for work."

I nodded, but I was feeling a little sad.

"If you leave now, you'll have plenty of time to get there in case it starts again."

I stared down at the floor. "Will you be around again? I mean... so we can talk again sometime?"

Granddaddy nodded. “I’ll be around. I don’t know when we’ll talk next, but I’ve been keeping my eyes and ears on you all these years. That’s not going to stop anytime soon. I promise.”

I smiled and nodded. “Cool.”

“And before I forget,” Granddaddy said reaching into his jacket. “Here’s something for you.”

I looked at what he handed me. It was a leather bound book, the leather soft and worn. When I opened it, all the pages were blank. I smiled at Granddaddy. “Thanks!”

“Okay!” Granddaddy exclaimed clapping his hands together. Then he jumped down from the picnic table in one quick motion.

I jumped down from too, but not quite as gracefully.

He clapped a hand on my shoulder. “Now remember what I said when we started talking. I don’t expect you to remember everything we talked about today. You’ll remember a lot of it, but even the stuff you don’t remember is in your mind now, so when you need it, it’ll be there for you.” Granddaddy looked around. “Okay… time to GOYA!”

I nodded, turned, and started to walk towards work. I took a deep breath and was surprised. The air did smell different than it had before.

“Hey… Dakota!” Granddaddy called out.”

I stopped and turned. “Yeah?”

“I’m proud of you. You’re a good kid.”

I beamed and nodded at him, and then started walking again. I was so full I could barely stand it. Then I realized I hadn’t thanked him and I really wanted to. I wanted to shake his hand and say thank you the way he’d shown me.

I turned and started jogging back to the pavilion, but he was gone. I stopped and listened, but couldn't hear anything other than the wind, the leaves, and the birds.

I was totally amazed that he could disappear so quickly and so completely. I knew there had to be a logical explanation, but I couldn't help but wonder if he'd just stepped out of this place and into that other world he goes to when he's not around. I still have no idea where that other place is, but I do feel like he left me with a bunch of clues for getting there.

My Journal

November 26th

Today was great. My head is still busting with all the stuff Granddaddy said to me. He gave me this book and I couldn't wait to write in it. I don't want to forget the things he said, so I'm going to write them here. I'll write the name of the first book I read here too. I don't want to forget it like Granddaddy did.

My girlfriend asked... rats! JENN asked me how things went today, but all I could say was that it was great. It's not that I didn't trust her enough to tell her about it. I'm just not sure how to explain it yet. I wanted to write down what I remembered first. Then maybe I'll be able to tell her about it.

Here's what I remember so far:

+ Remember people's names. It's a sign of respect.
+ Look for people to read about so I can learn more about how to be successful.
+ Everybody started out as a teenager, even successful people.
+ Keep making plans for your future.
+ Find a way to enjoy doing things I don't like to do.
+ GOYA... Get Off Your Ass!
+ Gratitude... I have to think about this one some more. I know what it is, but I haven't had much experience with feeling it, so I'm not

> sure I know what it feels like yet. I know how grateful I am that Granddaddy spent time with me today. Maybe I can use that as a reference point and build from there.

From what Granddaddy said, it sounds like I've been doing a pretty good job on my own. That was nice to hear. It's tough sometimes. At least now I have all the stuff Granddaddy said. I wonder if Colonel Reynolds is still alive. Granddaddy didn't say... but I didn't ask either.

I'm going to the library tomorrow to get my first book. I don't know what it will be yet, but that's okay.

Granddaddy also said he was proud of me. Never heard those words before.

About the Author

Dan Blanchard is an Award Winning Author, Speaker, Educator, two-time Junior Olympian Wrestler, two-time Junior Olympian Wrestling Coach, and a double veteran of our U.S. Military. He has successfully completed fourteen years of college, earned seven degrees, and teaches in Connecticut's largest inner-city high school.

He believes it is our duty to positively inspire and guide our youth every chance we get. *"It isn't fair to expect kids to know how to become citizens and leaders without help. It's up to us to help them."*

Dan has been employing this philosophy throughout his 20+ years as a teacher and coach. After repeatedly being asked by his students to write a book so other teens could hear what he was saying, he was inspired to sit down and write *Feeling Lucky?*

In addition to writing the "Granddaddy's Secrets" book series, Dan has been a featured guest on both radio and television, is one of the 10 people January Jones wrote about in her newest book *Priceless Personalities,* is one of the experts featured in parenting expert Bill Corbett's book: *The Expert's Guide to Teenagers,* is a Teacher Consultant for the University of Connecticut's Writing

Project, and was chosen by the *American Federation of Teachers* as their face and voice of educational reform.

You can contact Dan through his website: www.GranddaddysSecrets.com.

To Kathy---
stories!!! Tha

Sloane's Selection of Short Stories

by

Sloane Hawkins

Sloane Hawkins
Jeremiah 29:11

Sloane's Selection of Short Stories

By

Sloane Hawkins

PUBLISHED IN THE UNITED STATES

By

Aaron Book Publishing
Bristol, Tennessee
February 2009
Sales Orders (423) 212-1208
First Edition, First Printing

Cover Design: Kellie Warren-Underwood

Thanks to Meghan Hoss for the back cover photo.

Disclaimer

This document is an original work of the author. It may include reference to information commonly known or freely available to the general public. Any resemblance to other published information is purely coincidental. The author has in no way attempted to use material not of his own origination. Aaron Book Publishing disclaims any association with or responsibility for the ideas, opinions or facts as expressed by the author of this book.

Printed in the United States of America
Cataloging-in-Publication
ISBN: 978-0-9819195-6-0

Dedications and Acknowledgements:

Publishing a book has been a great experience for me, and I could not have done it without the help of the following people:

First, I would like to thank my publisher, Mr. Tim Rouse. He helped with the editing process, which I could not have done by myself. He is always very encouraging. Mr. Rouse spent a lot of time helping me with the title of the story, the cover and many other details that needed to be done to get this book ready. Thank you so much, Mr. Rouse, and everyone else on the publishing team.

Without my brother, who is a born comedian, I could not have written *Homerun Hawkins.* Much of the dialogue expressed in that story is exactly what he would have said in that situation. He really did play baseball, and many of the events actually did happen. He gave me a lot of funny ideas for that short story, and I hope you enjoy reading it. I laughed out loud as I read it back to myself. Thanks for being so funny, Reagan!!!

Of course, I have to thank my Mom and Dad for creating an environment that always encouraged reading and writing in our household. For this project, my Dad spent a lot of time proofreading the stories. My Mom read through every story and helped me edit. I could not have done it without you, Mom and Dad!

Another person I would like to thank is my 5th grade writing teacher, Mrs. Lori Massey. I wrote *The Magical Harp* as a school project, and without her, I don't think this story would be in this book. She helped me improve my writing skills and was always very inspiring. Thank you, Mrs. Massey!

My granddad, Bill Hawkins, is another person I would like to thank. He spent a lot of time editing *Larry the Ant and His Adventures.* He also helped both my grandmother and me operate the computer. His skills really came in handy, so thank you so much, Granddaddy!

Above all, I would like to thank my grandmother, Liz Hawkins, for spending so much time at the computer, editing and typing. This book started out as a grandmother-granddaughter project and ended up being so much more. Without her, I never would have been able to publish this book. She has been so much fun to work with and talk to. I'm glad she came up with the idea. Thank you, Grandmommy.

And, of course, thank you readers! I hope you enjoy my selection of short stories, and that you will keep an eye out for any more stories I write.

Thanks to everyone I listed on this page; I am really very grateful. This whole experience is something I will never forget and will carry with me for the rest of my life. You guys have made this year a very, very special year to remember!!!!

-----S.H.

Dedicated To . . .

Grandmommy. Thank you for this idea
and for always being there.
-S.H.

TABLE OF CONTENTS

Larry the Ant and His Adventures ***64***

Meet Larry, a mischievous ant who just wants to add more adventure to his life. So when he does something that he thinks will brighten his life up, he soon finds out that this was *not* the adventure he thought it would be. Now the question is, how will he get back home safely? Find out in ***Larry the Ant and His Adventures.***

The Magical Harp ***82***

Cody Thomas is one of the unluckiest kids in his school and town. So when he hears about a magical harp from his history teacher, he decides he must find this instrument. After all, it's supposed to bring good luck and fortune. But is this harp really what it's cracked up to be? Find out what happens to Cody and his sister in ***The Magical Harp!***

Double Trouble

"Jeremy Michael Johnson!" Jeremy's mother called from the bottom of the stairs. He winced. He hated getting up for school, especially on Monday. Jeremy's 7-year-old sister Jenna came in and started hitting him with her pillow. "Get up!" she shouted. He and his twin brother, Jake, stumbled out of bed. Today Jeremy's class was going to a farm. He hated chickens, ever since one pecked a scar into his arm. Jeremy was not looking forward to this trip, and told Jake that. "Yeah, that's what I wanted to talk to you about," he told him. He led Jeremy over to a corner. "I know how much you hate chickens, and you know how much I love them and every animal, so may-"

"No, no, no, no! I know what you're thinking, and there is no way. I am not switching places with you!" Jeremy exclaimed. "You remember what happened in kindergarten, don't you?" Jeremy was referring to the first – and the last – time they ever switched places. See, when you're an identical twin, and boy were Jake and Jeremy identical, you can sometimes trick people into thinking you are your twin, so you can switch places. They both have dark brown hair that falls in front of their eyes and curls up just a little near the ears, and light blue eyes with perfectly

tanned skin. In fact, if it wasn't for Jake's tiny mole right under his left eye, Mom and Dad probably wouldn't even be able to tell them apart! Anyway, in kindergarten, Jake and Jeremy decided to switch places, just to see what it would be like. They were caught right in the middle of finger-painting when Jake wouldn't answer the teacher when she said "Jeremy." He got in trouble for ignoring her, and then the beans were spilled. Mom and Dad grounded them like, forever, and they never switched places again.

"Yeah, I know, but I've got Mom's makeup to cover up my mole, and I promise, I won't forget I'm pretending to be you. Come on, Jeremy, we're in the 6th grade now!" Jeremy reluctantly agreed. Jake and Jeremy couldn't be more different. Jeremy was a straight--A student and always did his homework, while Jake got straight D's, and was always playing pranks on Jeremy, their Mom and Dad, and his teachers.

"Okay, but you can't say a thing about this. Not even to Austin!" Jeremy told Jake. Austin was Jake's best friend, and he was a prankster too. "Don't worry, Jeremy, it'll be fine. But you have to wear one of my shirts." Jake went into the laundry room and was back a second later with one of his NFL tee shirts. Jeremy took his polo shirt and handed it to him.

"Boys!" Mom called again. Jake and Jeremy looked at each other simultaneously, grinning at each other. No words needed to be said. It was a race to

the kitchen. Suddenly, at the same moment, they both took off down the stairs, both of them trying to be the first down.

"Okay, we've reviewed the plan. You got it?" Jeremy asked Jake. They were a block away from the school. "Yeah, Jeremy. I got it. Don't worry. I'll remember I'm pretending to be you." Jake assured him. Jeremy wasn't assured. "Okay, can I see your class schedule?" He handed it to him. "Science is first period. Don't be late. Mr. Hirsch is a real grouch," Jake told him. "I know, I have him, too." He was really nervous for Jake. Jeremy could pretend to be a trouble maker without getting into trouble, but he wasn't sure Jake could act like a good student. "There are the buses. See you later, Jake. Good luck!" he called after him. But he had already disappeared around the corner.

"Alright, let's see," Jeremy thought as he looked at his schedule. "I sure hope Jake and I can handle all this." With that thought, Jeremy took a deep breath and walked briskly to science class.

Mrs. Jamison and the bus driver were checking roll to be sure that everybody was present and ready to go visit the chicken farm. Jake took a deep breath and reminded himself to pretend he was Jeremy. He didn't want to cost himself or Jeremy any more trouble like he did in kindergarten. He answered the roll as Jeremy. So far he was off to a good start. He got on the bus along with the other students and took a seat with Scotty, one of his and

Jeremy's friends, but not one who knew every detail about them.

Jeremy, in the meantime, wandered into science and thought for a minute which seat was Jake's and when he remembered, he sat down. But then he thought about being Jake and knew he had to mess around with the other kids a little and see what kind of trouble he could start so no one would think he wasn't Jake. He went from seat to seat just being nosey and mainly horsing around until Mr. Hirsch got their attention and told them all to sit down and get ready for their pop quiz.

"Oh no!" exclaimed Jeremy, because he had no idea what the quiz would be on. Boy was he in trouble already and it was only first period!

Back on the bus, Mrs. Jamison decided they should review a bit before getting there, so she started asking questions. She knew Jeremy would know all of the answers because he was always on top of things and made great grades. "Please don't call on me!" thought Jake almost aloud. He became nervous, which was unlike him, so he sat very still as if he were Jeremy and hoping that the teacher would look past him. Naturally, that was too good to be true, as right then she looked straight at Jake and said, "Jeremy, can you name two reasons why most farms have chickens?" Jake swallowed hard and couldn't decide which was harder, coming up with the right answer or acting like Jeremy.

"Um, they lay eggs, um, um they um make sure the other animals are safe, and-" at that instant his teacher interrupted him. "Jeremy, I'm surprised," she said. "You know this. You're acting like your brother. Is everything OK?" Jake swallowed. "Ye-yeah," he stuttered. "I just haven't studied lately. We've been busy. Family stuff." Jake came up with that excuse. "Okay, keep working," his teacher said. Jake let out the breath he was holding as they arrived at the farm.

Back in science class, Jeremy had just realized something. Why would Jake get the answers correct? For goodness sake, he was *Jake*, after all! He didn't need to worry about getting the answers right. "Alright, class. Please answer the questions quietly, and you have 20 minutes to finish both pages. Start, now!" Pages rustled as the children quickly hurried to find the correct answers. The first question was *What is the name of the part of the brain that helps with your balance? "Easy,"* Jeremy thought. *"The cerebellum."* But Jeremy remembered that it would be like Jake to write the "balance part of the brain," so that's what he wrote. After 20 minutes, Jeremy had just finished one page. "Alright class, put down your pencils," Mr. Hirsch said. Jeremy reluctantly laid his down. Mr. Hirsch came by to gather the papers. "Jake, is this acceptable?" Mr. Hirsch demanded. "I think it is, sir," Jeremy answered. "This page will be your homework, Jacob," he told him sternly. "Finish it." Jeremy couldn't help but smile as the teacher

walked away. He had gotten away with pretending to be Jake. Oh, life was good.

On the other hand, the farm field trip was not looking good for Jake. He didn't know any of the questions his teacher asked him! He thought this would be fun, looking at the animals and all, but every time they stopped, Mrs. Jamison would ask him some weird question, like how many eggs does a hen lay a year?! Jake couldn't wait for the day to be over. It was the longest day of his life. When the field trip was finally over, Jake was ready to go back to being himself.

He met his brother at the bus stop so they could walk home together. To Jake's surprise, Jeremy was smiling from ear to ear. Jake had thought for sure Jeremy would have hated pretending to be the "not smart" twin! "What's up?" Jeremy asked Jake. Jake's jaw dropped down. "What do you mean 'What's up!'" Jake asked angrily. You're the smart one, so why are you pretending to like it?" Jeremy shrugged. "I'm not pretending. It's kind of cool not having to worry about studying all the time," he answered. Jake shook his head. He couldn't believe it! "I've had a terrible day," he told his brother. "What *are* the two reasons why chickens are kept in farms?" "That's easy," Jeremy replied. "They lay eggs for the farmer to eat and they hatch baby chicks so the farmer doesn't have to buy more." "Yes! I got one right!" Jake exclaimed. Jeremy rolled his eyes. "So, you wanna do this again tomorrow?" "Wait just a

minute, smarty pants, and let's talk about this first," frowned Jake, as he was considering the day he had just spent.

First of all, he wanted to know how Jeremy's day had gone, and what exactly he had missed in not going to class so some discussion was needed before he decided. Jake had really been miserable most of the day because of the questions Mrs. Jamison had always asked him and he could not relax and get into the mischief he enjoyed. However, on the other hand, it was kind of nice to be outside all day, being around the animals and learning more about nature but he did miss his regular friends. "Oh no, we could be in tons of trouble by now," thought Jake.

Meanwhile, Jeremy proceeded to give Jake his homework paper from the test in Science, as he gave out a big laugh. "That's just not funny," yelled Jake and he swung at Jeremy.

He continued, "When you change places with me, you are still supposed to be the smarty person that you are and not mess up on a test intentionally!" He could not believe Jeremy would do that to him and he was really angry at first. Then he thought that he just might turn the tables on Jeremy, and get him to do the homework if he could persuade him to change places at least one more day.

Jeremy thought about how he would handle being around his usual classmates the next day after Jake told him about Mrs. Jamison asking him so many questions that he didn't know. He knew his

friends would tease him about not knowing the answers so he wasn't sure he wanted to face them so soon. "Let's just try this one more time," Jeremy told Jake. Just then their mother came into their room, interrupting the boys' conversation.

"Hi boys," she said. Mrs. Johnson came around the corner and asked them about their day. "Jeremy, how did you like the field trip to a farm today? And did you get pecked by a chicken?" she asked. Wow! Jeremy and Jake exchanged quick glances back and forth trying to think about who would answer the question and not get mixed up. Before they could answer, she then looked at Jake and asked him what kind of mischief he got into that day. He thought, *Man, a mom always knows what to ask, even if we don't want to answer.* That was probably the quietest Jeremy and Jake had been all day.

Jeremy finally came up with an answer to say to his mother. "Um, yeah, it was great, Mom," he said. "I didn't get pecked, thank goodness!" Mom smiled. "No notes today, Jacob?" "No, Mom, is dinner almost ready?" "Yes, in about 10 minutes. Get ready." With that, Mom started walking down the stairs.

"Okay," Jake began, staring at his brother. "I don't want to be you. You're the smart one, so I can't be the smart one, and you need to be the smart one! I'm not changing smarts now!" Jeremy stared blankly at his brother. "I didn't catch that, and ***I'm*** the smart one." Jake rolled his eyes. "I don't want to pretend

to be you. I don't know anything about anything except sports!" At that moment Jenna came rushing into the twins' room. "Mom says to tell you dinner's ready. Oh, and Jeremy, your teacher sent you a note on the computer." Jenna skipped down the stairs. Jeremy and Jake slowly turned their heads toward each other. "I'm in trouble? I've never been in trouble in my life!" Jeremy exclaimed. The two boys ran down the stairs two at a time. "Hey, Mom, where's the note?" Jeremy asked as he slid into the kitchen. "Pulled up on the computer," she answered. Jake and Jeremy stumbled over to the family's laptop. Jeremy began reading aloud:

Jeremy Johnson,

Today at the farm I noticed that you didn't know the answers to many of my questions. On the bus you said it was "family stuff." Ever since the first day of school, I felt that you were paying too much attention to your school work, and not spending enough time with your family. I'm very glad to know you are. Just don't forget school! *Abigail Jamison*

Jake looked at Jeremy with a slight smile pulling at his lips. "Who knew?" he said. "I'm actually better at being you." "Uh, Mom, we're going to go wash up before dinner," Jeremy said as an excuse to get out of the kitchen so the boys could talk privately.

"I cannot believe this!" Jeremy exclaimed when they got into the bathroom. "Yeah, me neither. I cannot believe I can act just like me when I'm pretending to be you!" Jake said. "No, no, no," Jeremy told Jake, waving his hands. "You can't always be like you. If we're going to continue to switch places, you have to at least know a few answers!" "Fine," Jake agreed. "I'll do my homework and yours tonight." "Thank you," Jeremy said. "And I'll do your chores for the night." The boys gave their secret handshake, washed up, and sat down at the dinner table.

Everybody was enjoying dinner and chatting about ordinary stuff, but in the back of Jake's and Jeremy's minds lingered their plans for the next day. Each was deciding what they would do to prepare for school, and wondering if they could pull it off another day without getting caught. Jenna was being a normal kid sister, trying to get everyone's attention, so finally Jake and Jeremy talked to her about her day. That also caused the family to think everything was normal. After dinner and chores were completed, it was homework time. So Jake took out his homework sheets to complete and at times had to ask Jeremy for a little help. Maybe he was a little more serious than usual and actually did a good job on it.

The morning came early (as usual) and neither twin was ready to get up for school. "Come on boys. You are going to be late if you don't make those legs move," shouted Mrs. Johnson just as they

sat up in bed and stretched a bit. "Jake, are we ready to do this change "thing" again today?" asked Jeremy. "Well, yes, I guess so since I did all of that homework," replied Jake. Both were a little nervous since they would be at school all day today and have to dodge being close together with the possibility of being confused as the twin. That might cause them an awkward moment or two, but off they went to wait for the bus.

"Okay, Jake, I need the homework for first period and Mr. Hirsch," said Jeremy as he handed Jake his math book for first period. "Now you know how to do some of that math so try what you can and don't get an "F" for me," he said. "Now, Jeremy, you know I wouldn't intentionally mess up for you, don't you? After all, I guess we both need to do our best," Jake added. So they got on the bus and took a deep breath.

Jeremy took Jake's homework sheet into science class and handed it in to Mr. Hirsch. As he turned around to go back to his seat, Mr. Hirsch called out to him, "Jake, I am very pleased with this work you did and I want to compliment you on the change in your attitude lately. I knew that you could have done the test yesterday, and this shows me real progress in your ability to perform. I want to encourage you to keep working on that and let's see how much better your science grade will be." Jeremy stood there in a trance for a moment not knowing exactly what to say but remembered he had to change

his personality to Jake's so he smiled and thanked Mr. Hirsch without adding to it for now.

"Oh boy! What kind of trouble are we in now? Does this mean that I will ALWAYS have to be Jake now?" thought Jeremy. At least he was happy that Jake had gotten a compliment, but kind of doubted Jake would believe it. Well, first period was off to a great start for Jeremy or Jake or whoever he was!

Meanwhile, Jake was beginning to struggle a bit with the math lesson for today, but thank goodness Jeremy had helped him a little last night. Suddenly, Mrs. Gardner, the math teacher, looked at Jake and thinking he was Jeremy, asked him to go to the chalkboard and do some examples for the class. "Oh, man! What am I supposed to do now?" questioned Jake to himself. "Maybe they will pick out some easy equations to do and I can drag them out so the time will pass by quickly," he said quietly to himself. Slowly, he stood up and wandered up to the board and picked up the chalk waiting for his first problem. Then he had a very intelligent idea. "Mrs. Gardner, may I please make up some equations for the class to answer?" he asked. This way he would only use some problems that he could answer. She replied, "well yes, Jeremy. I think that is a good idea." So now Jeremy or Jake or whoever he is can breathe a sigh of relief also as his first period is off to a great start too.

Jake wrote on the board 49 divided by 7. "Um, Jeremy, we're learning exponents. Can you write 11 to the 9th power?" Mrs. Gardner asked. "Um, sure," Jake replied. He only knew a little about exponents. He thought about it for a moment, and then realized exponents were when you multiply 11 by itself 9 times! Jake almost moaned out loud, he was so depressed. "Mrs. Gardner, what is 11x11x11x11x-" Mrs. Gardner interrupted him. "That's what you're trying to figure out," she said. The class laughed. Jake glanced at the clock. It was only 8:40! Twenty more minutes until class was over! Jake had no choice but to pull the best prank ever pulled by middle-schoolers. He had to pretend to be sick. Jake grabbed his stomach moaning and fell to the floor. "Bad milk," he said, and then laid his head down. Right away Mrs. Gardner called the school nurse, Ms. Zoe Nelson. Ms. Nelson came rushing into the room and asked Jake if he could walk. Jake made a big show about standing up and followed Ms. Nelson to the office.

Jeremy had just gotten out of science class when the principal, Dr. Stands, called him down to the office. He gathered his books and walked down the long hallway to the office. He wondered what this could be about. He had never gotten called down to the principal's office in his life! But then again, he was sure Jake had. He pushed the office door open and walked in. "Mr. Johnson, the principal is waiting for you," said Ms. Preston, the secretary. Jeremy

opened the door to the principal's office. Dr. Stands was sitting at his desk. "Jake Johnson. Always a pleasure," he said extending his arm toward Jeremy. Jeremy could tell he didn't like Jake very much. "Son, your brother has gotten sick this morning. He said it was sour milk." Jeremy rolled his tongue around in his mouth. "Is he OK?" he asked. "We think so, but I called you down here to ask if you know anything about sour milk. We called your mother and she said she knew nothing about that.

"Is anything going on?" Dr. Stands asked. "No, but I can talk to him. Just nerves, probably. He has the huge, um, basketball game coming up this Saturday." "Jeremy plays basketball?" the principal asked. "I might have to see this huge game." "Uh, no sir, that's okay. I know you must be pretty busy," Jeremy objected. If the principal came to *Jeremy's* basketball "game" the boys would be toast! "Oh no, I love to get involved in my students' sports lives. What time is the game?" Dr. Stands asked. "Um, I'll call you," Jeremy told the principal. "Wonderful. Have a nice day, Jake." With that, Dr. Stands walked out of the office and to the secretary's desk. Jeremy slinked down in his seat. "Help me," he whispered to no one in particular. He was in a heap of trouble.

"Basketball?!?" Jake exclaimed after school that day. He had managed to get through the day without anyone suspecting he was Jake. "But you don't know anything about basketball!" "I know!" Jeremy told him. "I got confused about who was Jake

and who was Jeremy. What am I going to do?" "Well, it'll cost you, but I could pretend to be you. Austin plays 5 on 5 basketball and I'm sure he would let me join for one game. I'm not too good, but I know I can do better than you," Jake said. "Perfect!" Jeremy exclaimed. "Thank you, Jake." Jake rolled his eyes as Jeremy hugged him.

"Oh no!" Jake yelled. "What in the world are we going to do now to clear up this mess?" One thing we can hope for is that Dr. Stands will have something come up and keep him from attending the game, or else, I could give him the wrong time by mistake of course." Jake's brain was really working overtime trying to figure out some things.

Since the two boys' personalities were completely different, Jake was worried that Dr. Stands would be able to figure out which twin was which.

"The first thing I need to do is talk to Austin and make sure I can play on his team, just this once," he thought. That afternoon, as soon as the boys got home, Jake called Austin to ask about the basketball game.

He tried explaining his situation to Austin without telling him about the switching of him and Jeremy. He knew if he did, it wouldn't be a secret anymore and everybody in school would know about it. So he told Austin that he had a bet with his brother that he could play basketball and could make some baskets, but didn't have another team to play on. He asked if there was any way he could just play

on the team for that one game and Austin told him he would ask the coach and let him know.

Later that day, Austin called Jake to tell him it was okay for that one game because David was sick and would be absent and they really could use another player. However, he suggested to Jake that they meet at his house after school so Austin could practice with him and give him some team instructions. "Man, Aus, thank you so much for this!" Jake exclaimed. He was so happy he was able to play! The arrangements were made for Jake to meet Austin after school and Jeremy would tell their Mom what he was doing. So far so good!

Jake had never played in a real basketball game and all he had done was bounce the ball and shoot it at the goal, so Austin had a lot of coaching to do. Jake's sport was baseball, not basketball. After a few minutes, Austin wondered if he had gotten himself into a bigger project than he wished for because Jake was having a lot of problems making that big round ball go into the goal and through the net! However, Jake was still a lot better than Jeremy. As Austin and Jake found out, Jake was very good at lay-ups and free throws. After 20 free throws, Jake only missed three, and missed only one of 20 lay-ups.

As the day of the game neared, Jake got more and more excited. Basketball had become one of his favorite things to do.

Maybe Jeremy would practice with him at home too so he would learn faster, but Jeremy would

also have to help him with his homework. Jeremy wasn't too happy about that, but then he realized that he and Jake would be studying together for once. Maybe they would become closer buddies.

"Okay, Jake," Austin said the next day in Jake's and Jeremy's driveway. It was Wednesday, only three more days until the basketball game! Austin was showing Jake all of the basketball passes. He was working on the overhead pass. Jake held the ball over his head, brought it forward, and then let it fly. The ball zoomed over Austin's head, over the goal and almost hit the window! "Let's just stick with the bounce pass for now," Austin said to Jake. Jake agreed. They worked on passes and lay-ups for a while. Jeremy had to admit, Jake was looking a lot better. Friday night before the game, Jeremy called Dr. Stands. Jake had told him that he wanted to play in the game since he had practiced so much, so Jeremy gave Dr. Stands the correct times. Dr. Stands agreed to come at 11:00 Saturday morning. Jeremy hung up the phone feeling both nervous and excited for the game the next day.

"Alright, boys," Coach Zuckerman began the pre-game speech the next day at the basketball court. "You boys are very talented, just remember, if you are open, shoot! We're playing a great team today, so we need to do our best. Hands in!" The 8 boys all put their hands on top of the coach's and shouted, "1-2-3, COUGARS!!!!" The boys ran onto the court cheering. Jake wouldn't be starting. The Cougars

did very well in the first quarter and outscored their opponents by 9 points. At halftime they were leading 34 to 29, not a very comfortable lead.

After the coach's halftime speech, Jake started to play. He was nervous, but he swallowed it, and was ready to play. He felt like he could take anyone. Except Goliath, which is who he saw when he stepped out onto the court. Jake gulped and stared at his opponent. The kid was big; he must have been about 130 pounds. He was tall too, about 6' 1". Jake was suddenly not looking forward to this. "Play ball!" the referee said, throwing the ball into the air for jump ball. The big kid easily got it and dribbled down court. Jake tried to remember everything Austin told him about defense, but his mind was blank. He managed to stay in front of Goliath, but he ended up scoring anyway. The coach took him out of the game quickly after that.

In the 4th quarter the score was tied, 56 to 56. With 9 seconds remaining, Austin twisted his ankle so Coach Zuckerman sent Jake in for him. As Austin hobbled to the bench, he said, "Don't worry about that kid. Just stand right in his path and he'll run into you, which will be charging. You've gotten good at free throws." Austin patted him on the back and Jake hustled out onto the court. It was the Python's ball. Goliath got it, and ran to his goal. Jake closed his eyes and stood right in front of the kid. The next thing Jake knew, he was sprawled out on the court, stiff as a board, seeing stars. "Hey, Jake, are you

OK?" Coach Zuckerman asked, peering down at Jake from the court. Jake nodded and stood up. The ref handed him the ball. "Two free throws, kid," he said. Jake gulped and stepped up to the line. He glanced at the clock. Four seconds remaining, with the score tied at 56. Jake dribbled the ball twice, stared at the basket and threw the ball. It bounced on both sides of the rim, hit the back board, and bounced up. No good. The home team crowd groaned, and the visitors, the Pythons, cheered. Jake took a deep breath, dribbled the ball twice, concentrated on the goal, and took his shot. *Bounce, bounce, thunk, swish!* The last sound was the sound of the ball going through the net! Jake had won the game for the Cougars! The Pythons threw a one handed shot at their goal as time ran out, but it was no good. The Cougars had won, and all because of Jake! The team lifted him up on their shoulders, and shouted "Jake! Jake! Jake!" Jake was smiling from ear to ear, until Dr. Stands came over with Jeremy. They weren't smiling. "Hey, guys! We won! Thanks for coming, Dr. S!" Jake exclaimed. "Hey, Jake, great game, I just thought Jeremy was playing it," Dr. Stands said. Jake instantly stopped smiling. Was their cover blown? Jake would do all he could to save it.

The adrenalin was really flowing in Jake and he could hardly stand the excitement, but he was thinking about a solution to this problem before he spoke. Then he decided to stall a little and see how

far this excuse would go. "Well, Jeremy was really supposed to play but I persuaded him to let me have a try at it since I like sports and have never played basketball on a team before," he stated. "I might like to keep it up and play regularly on a team after today, as I enjoyed it a lot; that is, all except the bad case of nerves," he continued. Dr. Stands considered what Jake said and had to agree that it was very logical so he accepted that explanation. Jeremy was shaking his head "yes" the whole time hoping Dr. Stands would like that reasoning, which he did, and that would be the end of that discussion.

Jeremy was wondering if all this trouble was worth their having to make excuses, but he really didn't know what to do about it yet. After Dr. Stands left, Jeremy looked very sternly at Jake and grabbed his arm before he could take off running. "Listen to me, Jake, this arrangement has taken all kinds of wrong turns for us so far and I don't know where it will end," Jeremy said angrily. "Do you have any suggestions about what we need to do, or do you think it is about time to go back to being ourselves?"

Jake couldn't believe Jeremy was ready to throw in the towel, and after all, he was now ready to play basketball on a team full time. Should he beg Jeremy to continue to change places with him? Or should they try one more day and then decide if Austin's team would consider taking Jake on as a regular member? They would need to consider the pros and cons on the way home and decide what they

would do differently the next day to keep others from recognizing which twin was which. "Wait up, Jeremy, and let's talk about this before *YOU* make a decision without me," suggested Jake as they continued to walk home.

Jeremy was definitely the serious one who always made good decisions, except about changing places with Jake at school! Jake was a free-spirit personality who made hasty decisions without giving a lot of thought to them, or to their consequences. They might be identical twins, but only in looks and not in personalities. So while Jeremy was thinking of positive moves, Jake was only thinking about what he wanted to do, or what would be fun so their problem was in agreeing. No matter what Jeremy suggested, Jake would say, "But I want to play basketball again." They decided to talk with Austin before a final decision was made and if Jake could play ball on his team, then they would go on with the change for another day.

It was a bright and sunny morning that Monday, the last day the twins decided to switch places. Austin called Jake as soon as he woke up and told him there were only 3 more games in the season. Jake decided maybe he shouldn't continue on with the team. Unless, of course David was still sick on the next game. As the twins got ready for school, Jeremy just happened to glance at Jake's class schedule and saw that his class was supposed to go to the farm! Jeremy's eyes bulged out as he ran to tell Jake.

"Wow! Two days in one week!" he exclaimed. "That is, unless you want to go," he said jokingly to Jeremy. "No, thanks. So I guess this means we'll have to go back to our normal classes and act like ourselves," Jeremy said. "Yeah, I hope the school won't suspect anything," Jake said. "Yeah. Well, this has been fun. Have fun at the farm," Jeremy told his brother. And then the boys began getting ready for school.

Jeremy took a deep breath as he walked into math class for first period. He hoped he could act like Jake had the past few days. When Mrs. Gardner called him up to the chalk board to do some exponents equations, Jeremy tried to get 1 out of 3 wrong. When Mrs. Gardner popped a surprise quiz on the class, Jeremy did a little better because he didn't want Mrs. Gardner thinking he wasn't concentrating enough on school work. When she finally gathered the papers up, Jeremy was feeling pretty good about his day.

At the farm, Jake was acting, well, like Jake. He goofed off with his friends and didn't get any of the answers right his teacher asked him. The trip took up half of his day, so he went to science class afterward. Mr. Hirsch seemed to be paying special attention to Jake. It made him feel uncomfortable. After school, as Jake was packing his backpack, Dr. Stands' voice came over the P.A system. "Will Jacob and Jeremy Johnson please report to my office immediately? Jacob and Jeremy Johnson. Thank

you." The system crackled as he turned it off. Jake gulped. He hoped none of the teachers suspected anything. Jake slung his backpack over his shoulder and walked down to the principal's office.

When the principal's voice cackled over the P.A system and called for him to come, Jeremy was nervous. He hoped the teachers didn't know anything was up. He slowly picked up his books and headed over to Dr. Stands' office.

Jake and Jeremy got there at the same time and gave each other a weak smile when they saw the other. "Ah, there you boys are," Dr. Stands greeted them. "Jake, how did you enjoy your trip to the farm?" "It was good," Jake answered. It was obvious Dr. Stands was just doing some small talk. "Jake, do you have another basketball game coming up? Or are you going to be playing, Jeremy?" "Um, I might play tomorrow night," Jeremy answered. He was a little nervous. Where was this conversation going? "Excellent," Dr. Stands said. "I have informed your science teacher, Jake, and your math teacher, Jeremy, and they both want to see you play." Jeremy gulped. There was no getting out of this now, he thought. "Shall I be there at 7?" the principal asked. "That will work fine," Jake agreed. Jeremy stared at his brother as if to say, "Are you crazy?!?" But Jake just gave him a mischievous grin. Jake was definitely up to something.

"Jake are you crazy!?" Jeremy exclaimed as they were leaving school. "I can't play basketball!" "Exactly," Jake said. "I'm going to sub for you. David is still sick, so Austin said I could play tomorrow night. I'll make sure they'll call me 'Jeremy'." Jeremy was confused. "But---" he began. "Just wait and see," Jake interrupted. Boy, Jake was "the smart one" when it came to schemes.

The next day at the basketball game, Jeremy was sitting in the bleachers with Mrs. Gardner, Mr. Hirsch and Dr. Stands acting like Jake. Jake was down below acting like Jeremy. He had practiced basketball a lot on Tuesday, and Jeremy had to admit his brother had gotten very good at the game. His performance on the court proved it. He made 8 points that game, and the Cougars won easily, 41 to 32. It was a great game, and the teachers came down to congratulate him. "Hey Dr. Stands!" Jake exclaimed. "Great game, huh?" "Wonderful," Mrs. Gardner complimented. "Was it even awesomer than last game, Dr?" Jeremy winced at the bad grammar. "It was very good." Mr. Hirsch said.

"See you tomorrow!" Jake waved, and grinned at Jeremy. Jeremy grinned back.

The next Monday at school, right in the middle of social studies, Dr. Stands called the twins down to the office. Again. The two boys trudged down the hallway. They were their regular selves again. No more switching. Which is why both boys were surprised when the office was packed with Mrs.

Gardner, Mr. Hirsch, Mrs. Jamison, Dr. Stands, and Mr. and Mrs. Johnson. "Hey, what's up?" Jake asked, sounding just as surprised as Jeremy felt. "First off," Dr. Stands began. "Who is Jeremy and who is Jake?" The twins looked at each other, each deciding if they should say who they really were. They both agreed to be honest by the look on their faces. "I'm Jeremy," Jeremy said. "And I'm Jake," Jake said.

"We have called this meeting because of the way you two boys have been acting this past week." Jeremy and Jake gulped. "Boys, do you care to explain?" Dr. Stands asked them. Jeremy decided to tell the truth because he was tired of all the lies. He took a deep breath and told the whole story on why he and Jake had switched places. "We're sorry if we caused any trouble," Jeremy ended. "It certainly wasn't the easiest week," Mrs. Gardner said.

"Yes," Dr. Stands agreed, nodding his head, "and I agreed with Mrs. Gardner as well as Mr. Hirsch that you had switched at the basketball game when you said 'awesomer,' Jake."

"We're sorry," Jeremy apologized. "You boys may be identical, but you are not the same. Understand that," Mrs. Johnson told the boys. "Yes ma'am," the boys said in unison. "I hope a lesson has been learned here," Mr. Johnson said. "It has," Jake said. "We can't pretend to be each other because we're so different." "Exactly," the principal said. "And it doesn't really help your records. Maybe

for you, Jake, but not for you, Jeremy." Jake thought that was an insult, but he didn't say anything. "And if we hear of anymore of this switching business, there will be serious consequences." Dr. Stands added. "Yes sir," the boys said. "Thank you. You are dismissed." The twins walked out the door, and as they walked in different directions, they looked back at each other. They were both thinking of all they learned. They had become close friends in all of this. Jake nodded at Jeremy and gave him a slight smile. Jeremy smiled back and then they turned their heads and walked to their separate classrooms. Jake and Jeremy were two different kids, both with different interests. Never again would they pretend to be the other one. They were great just the way they were.

Hollywood Hopes

"Alright, Emma Crawford. You're up. Whenever you're ready," Mrs. Dawson told Emma. It was time for auditions for the school Christmas Pageant, and Emma Crawford was auditioning for the lead role, Priscilla Jones, a girl who wanted to find friends in time for Christmas.

"Bailey, please, I really need your help. Oh, come on. This would mean the world to me. I know it's Christmas Eve, but please come over and help me decorate my house for my parents." Emma read. The audience clapped and cheered. "Good job, Emma. I think our two finalists are Emma Crawford and Sydney Cross," Mrs. Dawson said, beckoning the kids to come onstage. "I'll let you know by tomorrow morning who will get the lead role." The crowd clapped and cheered again. Emma saw her two best friends, Chelsea Thomas and JD Hawk giving her the thumbs up sign. Emma grinned. "Alright, thank you to everyone for coming out here to audition. Have a wonderful afternoon, and I'll see you tomorrow in school. You are dismissed."

"That was great, Emma!" Chelsea praised on the way home from school. "Thanks, but I haven't gotten the role yet," Emma insisted. "You know you're going to get it," JD encouraged her. Emma smiled. This would be her big break if she got this role. Emma had been acting since she was eight years old, when her mother had signed her up for lessons. Since then, she had acted in a number of school and church plays, but none quite as big as this one. The Christmas Pageant at Harvard Middle School was the biggest event of the year. Every parent came to watch it on Christmas Eve night. Getting a large lead role as this one was a big deal to Emma.

"When do the rehearsals start?" Chelsea asked. She herself enjoyed acting, and was playing Bailey, Priscilla's friend in the play. "October 22nd," Emma answered. Today was October 21st. The group of actors would start rehearsing right after the lead role was announced the next day.

"Well, for sure I'll be there," JD told his friends. He didn't hang out with the girls as much as Chelsea and Emma did, but he would always be there for them. He liked to skateboard, play baseball, and chess.

"Well, this is where I leave," Emma said, turning to the right as Chelsea and JD kept walking straight. "See you guys tomorrow!" Emma called, leaping up the porch steps to her home. "Mom! Johnny! I'm home!" she called, setting her backpack

on the floor. "Hey, Em," Emma's fifteen year old brother walked into the room with a cookie in his hand. "Mom had to work late tonight, so it's just me and you for the rest of the day." Emma walked over to the cookie jar and grabbed a chocolate chip cookie. Just then the phone rang. "Hello?" Emma answered, her mouth stuffed with cookie. "Hello? Emma? This is Mrs. Dawson," the voice said. "Yes?" Emma asked, waiting for her to go on. "Well, I didn't want you and Sydney to have to wait all day, so I've made my decision on the lead part early. Congratulations, Emma. You have the part of Priscilla Jones." Emma spit out her cookie. "I do? Really? Thank you, Mrs. Dawson!" and then she hung up. "Johnny!" she screamed up the stairs. I got the part!"

Johnny lazily answered Emma but really couldn't get too excited since drama just wasn't his thing. Of course he was happy for Emma though and gave her a "high five" along with "good going, sis!" She sat down on his bed to talk a minute about the play while she finished her cookie. She explained to him about the main theme and could hardly wait for her Mom to come home so she could share in her excitement. Johnny asked about the other actors and actresses and pretended to care for Emma's sake so she still felt very excited about getting the part.

As their Mom came through the door, she yelled out, “Emma, Johnny, I'm home!” Emma came bounding down the stairs, taking two at a time and yelled, “Mom, I got the part in the school play that I tried out for!! Can you believe it?” Her Mom picked her up and twirled her around the floor she was so excited for her and gave her a big hug for congratulations. Now, the big question facing Emma is-- “Do I tell anyone else that I got the part now or should I just wait and let Mrs. Dawson tell them?” She really wanted to tell someone but didn't want to disappoint Sydney so it was a very difficult decision for her to make. Just then, the phone rang and Johnny called down to Emma that it was for her. She reached for the phone, still wondering what to do about telling someone she got the part.

“Hello?” she said into the receiver. “Hi, Emma. This is Sydney,” the voice said. “Hi,” Emma greeted her. “I just wanted to tell you congratulations on getting the part of Priscilla,” Sydney said nicely. “Thanks, Sydney. Thanks a lot.” “You're welcome! I got the part of Lauren, Priscilla's sister, so we'll be seeing a lot of each other.” Sydney told Emma. “That's great! I'm happy for you!” Emma exclaimed. See you at rehearsals tomorrow.” “Yeah, see ya,” Sydney said, hanging up the phone. *Well, that was nice*, Emma thought. *Oh, I just can't wait for rehearsals!*

*** *** *** *** *** *** *** *** *** *** *** ***

"Alright, Emma, from the top," Mrs. Dawson told Emma the next day at rehearsals. Emma had her long, wavy brown hair in a tight ponytail, and was wearing her new green Christmas shirt her mother had bought her. Emma thought it brought out her dark green eyes. "It's almost Christmas! Oh, man, I wish I had a friend to give a gift to!" Emma acted out mournfully. "You can give it to me," Sydney said, pretending to be Priscilla's sister. "Good job girls," Mrs. Dawson interrupted. "I think you have that part down pretty well. Chelsea, Jake, can you start in the middle of Act 3?" "Sure," Jake Acker said. He was a very talented actor, and if he was a girl, Emma felt sure he would have beaten her out of the lead part.

"Hey, Bailey! Did you do anymore research on our history report?" Jake asked. "No, Josh, for the last time, you have to help me work. Even though it's almost Christmas vacation," Chelsea told Jake.

"Great job, kids. It's almost 5:00, so you are dismissed. Way to go!" Mrs. Dawson praised. Emma and Chelsea hurried down the stage. "Great job, girls!" JD said, giving them a hug. "You guys are so ready for Opening Night!" "Thanks, JD, I hope we are!" Emma said laughing.

*** *** *** *** *** *** *** *** *** *** *** ***

After two months of exhausting rehearsals, the group finally was ready for Opening Night. On

December 24th the group of actors met backstage at the school auditorium. Emma peeked out from behind the curtain. There had to be at least 200 people in the audience. Emma gulped nervously.

"Alright, kids. You've worked long and hard for this," Mrs. Dawson began. "You know your lines by heart, and I feel sure you will do an incredible job. If you forget your lines, don't panic, just look at me. So go out there and give it your best!" The group cheered, and headed out onto the stage. "It's almost Christmas!" Emma began. The kids finished out the play perfectly, with no mistakes at all. When they were done, the crowd gave them a standing ovation. Emma and everyone else had to bow 4 times! After the curtain finally closed, the kids gave each other high fives and hugs all around. There was laughing and cheering and clapping too. "Great job, boys and girls! You guys did incredible!" Mrs. Dawson raved. "I'm so proud!" JD came backstage and congratulated the girls. "By the way, Emma," he said. "Your parents wanted me to tell you that there's someone out there who wants to see you. They say it'll be the best Christmas present in the world."

Emma felt a little scared and very excited, not knowing who could be out front waiting to see her. Everyone wanted to speak to her, hug her, and congratulate her so the immense crowd made it very difficult to move around and make her way out to the front. When she finally did reach her parents, there

was someone there who she didn't recognize but her dad introduced him to her. "Emma, this is Mr. Wright from Wallace State Jr. College School of Drama. He was invited to attend the school play because he wants to be aware of the local talent and keep up with students who might want to attend the college when they graduate," said her dad. Emma was so excited, she didn't know what to say. "Oh, oh, Mr. Wright, I am so happy to meet you," exclaimed Emma. "And I am very pleased to meet you, Emma, and I am especially happy to see the amount of talent in your school. I want to stay in touch with you and hopefully, you can perform in some of our college dramas to give you experience if you would like. I think you are a natural in acting and would be happy to grant you a scholarship toward some college courses that you can be taking along with your high school courses." Mr. Wright explained as she listened closely. "Really? Are you serious? Oh, Mr. Wright, that is the best news I have ever received!! Do I need to audition soon?" asked Emma. "Yes," Mr. Wright replied. "If you want to come to the college on January 3rd, that would be wonderful. You could meet some of our very talented girls, and Mrs. Johnson, who runs the school, could give you some pointers. A few of our extremely talented have gone on and been in a few movies and guest starred in some TV shows." "Really? That's great!" At that moment, JD and Chelsea came over. "Hey, Emma! The whole

group's going over to get some ice cream. Want to come?" "Sure!" Emma said enthusiastically. "Bye, Mr. Wright. And thank you! It was great to meet you!"

*** *** *** *** *** *** *** *** *** *** *** ***

Every day until January 3rd, Emma practiced the lines she was going to say at the drama college. When the big day finally came, Emma was so excited she could hardly contain herself. "Mom! Dad!" she called from the stairs. "I'm ready to go!" "Okay, Emma!" her mom called back. "Go ahead and get in the car!" Emma did as she was told and soon they were headed to the drama college.

"Hi, Emma!" Mr. Wright greeted her at the door. "Come in. I want you to meet Mrs. Johnson and Olivia Dewberry, one of our actresses." Emma said good-bye to her mom and followed Mr. Wright through the doors. "Mrs. Johnson!" Mr. Wright called as a lady that looked to be in her mid-forties, walked down the hall. She had long, brown hair that was turning gray at the ends. "Yes, Howard?" she said wearily. "Ma'am, this is Emma Crawford, the young girl I told you about who was in her school Christmas play." "Oh yes!" Mrs. Johnson's blue eyes lit up as she recognized the name. She put out her hand for Emma to shake. "Mr. Wright has told me quite a lot about you, Emma. I wish I had been at the play myself," Mrs. Johnson said. "Yes ma'am," Emma replied, "it was a lot of fun." "I'm

glad. Come on over here. I'll introduce you to Olivia Dewberry, one of our talented young actresses," added Mrs. Johnson.

Emma followed Mrs. Johnson and Mr. Wright through the halls. They were long halls, kind of like the ones at her school. Badges and posters and pictures of young girls draped the walls, so you could hardly see the mahogany wall paneling.

"Olivia!" Mrs. Johnson called, as a girl who looked to be about 17 years old stepped out of a dressing room. "Yes ma'am?" she asked, stopping in the hall. Olivia had honey blonde hair and shiny brown eyes that sparkled. She had a script in one hand and a pen in the other.

"Olivia, this is Emma Crawford. She's the girl that was in her school's Christmas play. She had the lead part," Mrs. Johnson explained to Olivia.

"Oh, it's very nice to meet you, Emma," Olivia said, offering her hand for Emma to shake. Emma shook it. "Olivia, we were hoping you could arrange for Emma to be the eleven-year-old little sister of Phoebe, if that's possible. We want her to get the experience," Mr. Wright explained. "Sure," Olivia answered. "She needs to be a quick learner, though, because our play's in a month and a half. In two weeks, Alicia Eckstein is going to come over and watch the rehearsals. Emma, do you think you could memorize two or three acts in two weeks?" "Sure!" Emma agreed. She had a great memory. "But, who is Alicia Eckstein?" "Ms. Eckstein is an agent for a

lot of our young actors and actresses today. After three weeks of starting a new play, Ms. Eckstein comes to check it out. She'll choose the most talented actors to possibly go on to movies and TV shows in Hollywood," Mrs. Johnson informed Emma. "Cool!" Emma exclaimed.

Olivia told Emma to come with her and they would begin to write Emma's part. "This is so exciting I can hardly contain myself!" exclaimed Emma, "and I surely didn't think I would be involved in writing the script." Olivia was so kind and patient and seemed like a professional already. She explained the play, the characters, setting, and the whole project to Emma. Emma was so interested in the whole thing that she couldn't believe it when it was time to leave for the day. Emma's head was swimming; there was so much information in it from one session with Olivia. She suddenly felt really exhausted! She wondered aloud if this was just a big dream or if it actually happened. Now she had to concentrate on what she might add to the play for her character to be involved in, so she brought a copy of the script home with her to study. She would bring some ideas to Olivia when they met again for writing.

Mrs. Crawford was waiting for Emma when they were finished and was anxious to hear all about the meeting with Mr. Wright and the others involved in the play. Emma was so excited she tried to start at the beginning, but kept jumping over some of the

facts to get to the end. Finally, she shouted, "Mom, guess what?! I met this girl named Olivia who is writing the play and she wants me to help her write my part!! Can you just believe it? I can hardly wait to get started making notes so I can learn my part and maybe Alicia Eckstein will choose me to go to Hollywood." They talked all the way home, until Emma fell asleep in the car from excitement and exhaustion, with her brain full of wonderful ideas.

*** *** *** *** *** *** *** *** *** *** *** ***

The next day after school, JD and Chelsea met Emma at the drama college. "This is so cool!" JD was in awe of the huge stage with a red velvet curtain and beautifully polished wood floor. "Emma, I wish I were in this play!" Chelsea exclaimed. "Hey! There you are, Emma!" Olivia greeted her. "Ready to get started?" "Yeah, I sure am!" Emma said. "You guys wait here," she told her friends. "I should be done in about an hour." With that, Emma scurried to the stage with Olivia.

"Okay, Emma, we wrote one act of Allison for the play. Do you have any more ideas?" Olivia asked. "Yeah, I do," Emma began. "I was thinking she should maybe pull some pranks on Phoebe, you know, being the mischievous little sister she is." "Fantastic!" Olivia exclaimed. "I love it!" And for an hour, the two discussed ideas on Allison, the kid sister of Phoebe, the main character. As JD, Chelsea, and Emma walked home together, Chelsea

said, "So when is this Alicia Eckstein coming to watch the play?" "In. . . oh my goodness! She's coming over next week! I have to work on the acts!" Emma said. "Did you finish writing them?" JD asked. "Yeah, I just need to memorize them," Emma replied. "Bye, guys. See you tomorrow!" she said, as she took off down the street.

For the whole week, Emma was constantly rehearsing her lines for the play. She practiced them in between classes in school while her friends rolled their eyes. On the day when Ms. Eckstein was scheduled to come, Emma felt as ready as she could be.

"Alright, guys. You are ready for this," the director, Mrs. Johnson, said before the curtain opened. "We will only do three acts because that's all Emma's had time to rehearse. Go get 'em!" The kids cheered and headed out onstage. In the play, Emma portrayed the eleven-year-old little sister of Phoebe, always getting into trouble. That character was so unlike Emma it was a challenge to play her. But she did it perfectly and after the play, Ms. Eckstein called her over. "Emma Crawford, is that right?" Ms. Eckstein greeted Emma. "Yes ma'am," said Emma politely. "You are a very talented young girl," she complimented. "Now, this isn't a snap decision, and talk to your parents about this, but I believe there is a great deal of potential in you for acting." "Thank you," Emma said. "A group of writers from Hollywood have created a new TV series

called *Country Cousins*," Ms. Eckstein explained. "We are still looking for actors, and you would be perfect for the twelve-year-old girl, who is tricky, funny and sensible. Her name is Abby Jackson." "Oh, I would love to play her!" Emma said. Finally, after all these years, someone was offering her a job as an actress in Hollywood! "Wait. Talk to your parents, decide if it's right for you, then give me a call," Alicia said, handing Emma a card with Alicia's picture and phone number. "And great job," she said as she walked away. At that moment, JD and Chelsea ran over. "We only heard the last part," JD said, breathing hard, "but it sounds great. You're starring in a TV show?!?!" The friends began celebrating. "Not yet," Emma told them. "I still have to ask Mom and Dad, but I'm pretty sure I'm acting in it!"

*** *** *** *** *** *** *** *** *** *** *** ***

Mrs. Crawford met Emma at the door and could see that she was all smiles as she came inside. "Well, dear, how did the audition go today with Ms. Eckstein? Was it what you expected and how did you do?" asked her mother. Again, Emma was so excited she hardly knew where to begin. She said, "Oh, Mom, I can't believe how much fun and how rewarding it is to help write a story and then act it out like I'm doing in this play! I know this is what I want to do for the rest of my life and I might never have known that if I didn't have this chance given to

me by Mr. Wright." She hugged her mom and then told her what Ms. Eckstein had said about her talent and acting in Hollywood. She waited for a reply from her mother but noticed a slight delay in her reaction. Suddenly, Emma became a little nervous that her mom and dad might not permit her to go to Hollywood, so she asked her what she thought about that possibility.

Mrs. Crawford was very careful and thoughtful before she spoke and then she looked right into Emma's eyes. She told Emma how much she and Mr. Crawford loved her and how they both only wanted the very best for her for all of her life and not just for the moment. She explained to Emma that sometimes we really don't know what is best for us, and we think that because we want something so badly, it must be real but actually that is not always the right thing. "Don't be disappointed because I don't know at this moment what is best for you or us but I do want you to consider seriously what I am saying to you. Then know that your dad and I have to discuss this some more before we can give you our answer," stated Mrs. Crawford. "And before we make our decision, we will have to know more about this adventure to Hollywood for our daughter, including what it involves as far as the length of time, and what you would be doing while there. We would actually need to have a meeting with Ms. Eckstein to work out all details before we can agree or disagree," she said.

She knew it would be a wonderful opportunity for Emma, but there was a great deal of responsibility for them as her parents before a decision could be made. She encouraged Emma not to be upset but just to be patient until the details could be worked out and then their decision made. Even though Emma knew her parents well and what they expected of her, she was a bit disappointed to have to wait for an answer. She tried to persuade her mom that it would all be okay and she could just say "Yes, it is okay," but she decided to give her parents a little time before she started to plead with them. Just maybe she was a little relieved that this would give her a little extra time to think about exactly what "going to Hollywood" meant and how it might change her life.

*** *** *** *** *** *** *** *** *** *** *** ***

"Emma, can you come down here, please?" Emma's father called from the dinner table. Right after a hearty meal of steak, corn and mashed potatoes, her parents had told Emma to go upstairs while they discussed what to do about Emma's big break in Hollywood.

"Emma," Mr. Crawford said, resting a hand on her shoulder. "Johnny says you should go for it. What do you think?" Emma nodded her head quickly. "I want to go!" she told her parents. Mr. and Mrs. Crawford looked at each other. "I don't want her to turn into all those actors you hear about

on TV," Mrs. Crawford said to her husband worriedly. "Don't worry, Mom," Emma assured her. "I know right from wrong. I'll be fine." Mr. Crawford bent down so he was eye level to Emma. "Emma, I know you want to do this. But, if we hear of one thing you do wrong in Hollywood, we are taking you out. For good." Emma jumped into the air and hugged her parents and her brother. "Oh, thank you!" she exclaimed. "I promise I'll be great!" Emma ran up to her room, "yahooing" all the way.

A few days later, after the family had called Ms. Eckstein, it was arranged that she would be Emma's agent. After a week, Emma had tried to learn everything there was to know about acting. Don't worry if you make a mistake, they can edit that out. Get to know your fellow actors, because they could be with you from one season to ten. Always listen to your director; he's like an umpire in a baseball game. On February 2nd, Emma was all set to head out into her plane and go to Hollywood.

Her friends and their parents, along with Johnny, Mr. and Mrs. Crawford, Ms. Eckstein, and of course, Emma, flew all the way from Harvard Middle School in Hartford, Connecticut to the Recording Studios in Hollywood, California.

"I'm so excited!" Chelsea said as she took her seat in the plane. "Remember, Emma, you haven't gotten the part yet. You and four other girls

are trying out for the role of Abby," Ms. Eckstein reminded her. "Yes, absolutely," Emma replied.

When the group finally arrived in California, Emma felt as ready as she could be. The next day, she would audition for a major role in a soon-to-be famous TV series!

The Crawfords stayed in a nice hotel a block away from the Studio, while the Hawks and the Thomas' stayed right next door. Right away, Emma practiced her emotions in front of a mirror. She was ready.

The next morning, at 9 o'clock sharp, Emma met Ms. Eckstein at the audition part of the Studio. "Don't be nervous," Ms. Eckstein told her. "You know this." Emma headed out on to the stage. The other girls were good. Really good, Emma thought. Ms. Eckstein said all of them had been in a lot of other movies. As soon as her name was called, Emma took the stage. It was between her and another girl, Hailey Anderson, whom Ms. Eckstein said had been in a lot of movies. Finally, after about 15 minutes, the judges made their decision. "Ms. Emma Crawford, you will play the part of Abby Jackson in *Country Cousins,"* the male judge said. And after that, it was pandemonium. JD and his family went nuts, while Chelsea came over and gave her a hug. Ms. Eckstein told Emma "good job," and the rest of the Crawford family didn't do anything. They were too awestruck. Emma did the same. Finally, her dream was coming true, and she

didn't know how to react. "Thank you," she finally managed to spit out to the judges, and then went to celebrate with the rest of her friends and family.

Emma decided not to celebrate too much yet. She was very intelligent, along with talented, so she figured she would just play it cool for now. She was indeed happy and excited but wanted to read the rest of the story to get a grip on the whole episode before starting to learn her lines. Even though she wasn't really from the country, she had cousins and friends so she could relate to the production. She still couldn't believe she was in Hollywood until the production staff gave her the taping schedule! "Wow," she said, "When do I have time to sleep or eat?" The full schedule was overwhelming; Emma knew now why one has to be a bit special and a quick learner to be able to tape that quickly.

Mr. and Mrs. Crawford and a few of her friends decided to stay in Hollywood for a few days to help Emma get adjusted to her new endeavor and schedule and to be sure she would be happy there. Emma's first appointment was to meet with the production staff and the different actors just to become acquainted. She was a very friendly and out-going person, so none of this affected her too much at all. Once she met the actors playing directly with her, she knew more about the role and how to play it. Her confidence level increased rapidly, which encouraged her to begin immediately learning lines.

Ms. Eckstein, as Emma's manager, was always nearby to help her in any way she needed. This security helped the Crawfords to feel Emma was in good hands. They could now return to Connecticut and resume their lives as the parents of Emma Crawford of Hollywood portraying the part of Abby Jackson in *Country Cousins.*

Emma was sad for her friends and family to leave but she didn't have time to dwell on that. Production would start on February 9th and she had lots to do before then. Her manager helped direct her in studying lines, learning the setting of the play, and feeling comfortable with the total experience. She worked hard and learned fast and on February 9th, she arose early and prepared for her first appearance in *Country Cousins.* "I know I will do a good job and then I will be ready for my second performance in Hollywood," she exclaimed. One thing she needed to do was to write letters to Mrs. Dawson, Sydney, Mr. Wright, and Olivia to especially thank them for their guidance and leadership in pursuing her dream of a lifetime. And of course, she would write her parents and good friends from home too, so she could stay in touch with them also. Her appearance time on set was 8 a.m. on the 9th and she arrived early at 7:30 so she would be there and ready to start right on time.

As she approached the door, she stopped, sighed, and said "I just can't believe that I made it to Hollywood. Now I have to prove that I can finish my

task, do a great job, stay the same person I am, and move right up to the next level so this will be my home for a long time." Then, Tyler Aarons walked in. He was an actor who had been in two other movies and would be playing AJ, Abby's twin in *Country Cousins.* "Hey, Emma," he greeted her. "Hey," Emma said back. And then, suddenly to her surprise, JD and Chelsea and Emma's parents walked on the set! "Mom, Dad, what are all you guys doing here?" Emma exclaimed joyfully. "We wanted to surprise you. You didn't really think we would miss your first filming day, did you?" JD said. Emma went and hugged her friends and family.

At that moment, the director, Jacob Mann, William Brown, and Zoe Worth walked into the room. They were all other actors of the TV show. "Alright, kids, have you reviewed your lines?" David Austin, the director asked. "Yes!" the kids said back. Then they all took their places. "Alright, Jacob," Mr. Austin began. "You have the first line, at the car in the driveway." "Yes, sir," Jacob replied, hurrying to his place. He would be playing the oldest child in the series, Nick Jackson. "And, and action!" he shouted. "Hey, Soph," Jacob began. "Hello, Nicholas," Zoe, who played Sophie, replied coldly. Her character was a girl who was an only child and had to move in with her 4 cousins in the country. Emma's part wouldn't come till much later, but when it did she felt she'd be ready. She played a tomboy, the only girl in the Jackson

household, until of course, Sophie moved in. There were a lot of bloopers, and Emma was enjoying every minute of it. The way the cast laughed about the mistakes, and the way Mr. Austin was so easygoing. After about an hour, rehearsal was finished. They would have a live audience on Friday, five days from then, because it was a comedy.

"Great job, kids. Take 5," the director said after rehearsal was finished. "Awesome, Emma! That was so cool!" JD exclaimed when it was over. "Way to go," Ms. Eckstein told Emma. Emma felt she had done an awesome job, and was quite proud of herself.

*** *** *** *** *** *** *** *** *** *** *** ***

After the episode was released to the public, Emma received all sorts of fan letters saying how much they loved the new TV series. Emma wrote back to each one. Soon, her name was all over Google, her face was all over MySpace, and her movies and TV series were all over YouTube. She was the rage of Hollywood, and she hardly had time for school.

Just recently, Mr. and Mrs. Crawford agreed that Emma was too popular to go to a regular public school. So, Mrs. Christansen, an older, experienced teacher, agreed to tutor Emma for 3 hours a day, 4 days a week. Emma was an excellent student, even with the chaos of being a huge actress. She had acted in 3 movies, all adventure ones. Ms. Eckstein

thought that Emma was fantastic at thinking how she would act as if she was in that situation. Finally, on April 8th, Emma got her big break. She was asked to act in a movie about identical twins! "But I don't have an identical twin," Emma told Ms. Eckstein. "That's the magic of production," Ms. Eckstein told Emma. "You have to play both parts, and then they double it, so it seems as if two different people are playing the identical twins, but really it's only one." She explained.

The Crawfords and JD and Chelsea had come again to see Emma."Wow," Chelsea awed as she walked into the studio. "Cool, isn't it?" Emma asked her friends. "Cool? Try incredibly awesome!" JD exclaimed. "I can't wait to see how you do in your movie!" Emma ended up doing quite well, even though this was a new experience for her. Tyler, Zoe, and all the other cast members in *Country Cousins* came to watch her.

The movie, *Twin Titans,* was highly successful when it was released. Emma had had so much fun acting in it. Soon, as she got older, she planned to focus on just *Country Cousins.* It was still in production. Emma had become so close with her cast mates, she was extremely sad three years later, when they finally decided to call it quits. Emma was still quite famous, and recently, she had been called to appear on Regis and Kelly, the Late Show with David Letterman, Larry King, and many other talk shows.

Emma began to slowly stop enjoying all her fame, which surprised her, because she had always loved acting. Maybe it was just the fact that Emma had grown up and had missed out on part of her childhood. She decided to slow down and still act, but only when she wanted to. Her talent was in great demand and she could pick and choose whatever she wanted to work in. However, she wanted to just take a break away from working and return to Connecticut for some catching-up time with her dear friends and family. "Oh what wonderful memories I will take with me for the rest of my life or until I act again!" exclaimed Emma as she boarded her private plane to return home. Emma Crawford was now a household name from Hollywood!

The End?

"Emma!" her mother called from the bottom of the stairs. It was four years later, and Emma was 16. Her brother was 19, and had just recently gone to college.

"Yes?" Emma called back. "Ms. Eckstein wants to talk to you. She's on the phone!" Emma still kept in touch with Ms. Eckstein, although she had only guest starred in a TV show since she had left Hollywood.

"Yes, Ms. Eckstein?" Emma said when she picked up the phone. "Emma, I understand that since you left Hollywood, you have become the

number one writer in your high school." Ms. Eckstein said to Emma. "Yes, ma'am," Emma replied. It was true. Emma had won numerous awards at school for her creative writing. She had entered 4 competitions, winning three, and coming in second for one. "Well, you remember Mr. Austin, the director for *Country Cousins,* right?" "Of course," Emma said. "Well, I sent him one of your essays, and he was so impressed with how you made it funny, dramatic, and interesting all at the same time, that he wants you to come back to Hollywood and write for his newest production, *The Adventures of Sierra Lee.* Would you like to?" Emma thought about the situation. She left Hollywood because she didn't like all the fame and wanted to get back to normal life. But she could write at home! She discussed it with her parents and they agreed. "Sure, Ms. Eckstein. I'd love to!" Emma exclaimed.

So from that day until college, Emma wrote for the *Adventures of Sierra Lee,* and enjoyed every minute of it. Emma Crawford, Actress, was now Emma Crawford, Writer. *Man, you really can have it all,* Emma thought.

THE END

Sloane Hawkins

Home Run Hawkins

One out. Runners on third and first. Fifteen to twelve, we were losing, and I was up to bat. My coach came by and said, "No pressure, Reagan, but we need a hit." I felt nervous, and like I was going to hit it. I did. A single down the third base line. The runner on first advanced, and the runner on third stayed put. That hit later won the game for us, 16 to 15, our favor. The most exciting game I've played all season long against the Cubs. Go Dodgers!

*** *** *** *** *** *** *** *** *** *** *** ***

"Mom, where are my shoes?" I called up the stairs. It was the first baseball practice and everyone was going nuts! My sister was packing my bat bag, my Dad was just coming home from work, and Mom was upstairs folding clothes, probably. That's what she's always doing. And, as usual, Yukon was barking his head off.

"Maybe where they're supposed to be, honey?" my Mom called back. I laughed. "Mom, you crack me up." I never put my shoes where they're supposed to go. I looked under the foosball table, and sure enough, they're there! I tried to put

them on, but they were cleats, and I couldn't tie them. "Yukon!" I shouted, his barking finally getting on my last nerve, as Mom always said. He ran down the stairs with his favorite toy, a soccer ball, hoping someone would play with him. "Sorry, boy, see ya," I said, kissing his head. I finally got my shoes tied and ran outside.

"Hey, Sis," I said to Sloane, my sister, but I just call her Sissy. "Where's your bat?" she asked me. I found it in the back of the truck and handed it to her. "Well, there's Dad," I said, grabbing my bag. Sissy hopped in the car with me as we headed out the driveway.

"How was school today?" Dad asked. "Good," Sissy said. "I got 100% in Science!" We're home schooled, I should probably mention. It might be important. Soon we pulled into a parking lot at OC Taylor Elementary School. We would be practicing on that field. I hopped out of the car and Sissy said, "I'm not carrying the bag. It's your practice." Geez, she can get so grouchy sometimes. She's probably just jealous. (I wish). When we finally got to the field, my new coach, Stan Addison, said "hi" to me. Sissy got on her glove like me and went to play catch. When another kid got there, she moved and I played catch with him. His name was Ethan. I was kind of nervous when I went to practice, but it was fun when I learned everyone's names. There's Landon, Adam, Ethan, Will, Ben, Collin, Rhett, Brendan, Mark, and me. The first

practice was so much fun. I think Will is my new best friend. I can't wait until my first game. I learned a lot of basics at that first practice, but I was really tired from swinging the bat, throwing the ball, and especially running around the bases.

We were scheduled to play our first game on Friday night and wouldn't you know, it rained crazily that day so of course our very first game was cancelled! What a disappointment that was! I was really excited about actually playing a game and hoped it would stop raining but when the time came, we were notified that "No Game Tonight". Oh well, I guess I can practice with my Dad, who is also one of our coaches, over the weekend and be ready for the next game on Tuesday, but I am not very happy about this. Sissy said she would throw to me and let me hit some and Dad could teach me a little about watching the ball, and making sure I could catch one hit to me in the field so I guess that was better than nothing.

I counted the days until game day again and begged it not to rain it out again. Seems like the days go so slowly when you can't wait to do something exciting, like play your first baseball game. Well, Tuesday arrives and guess what? There's no rain today so I asked Mom if my uniform was all ready and I patiently waited for game time.

I didn't know what position I would play tonight because we were changed around so we could play each position during the season. I would

just have to wait until tonight. As the time nears, I want to make sure everyone is ready and I won't be late. "Sissy, would you help me put my equipment in the bat bag and make sure all of my uniform is ready to go?" Then, I had a long talk with Yukon about me playing a good game, and he licked me for good luck and wagged his long red tail which I knew meant he wanted to go too. I said, "Sorry, big boy, you need to stay home and wait for me to finish my game and I'll tell you all about it then." Yukon is my best buddy and we understand each other.

"There you are," Coach Stan said when I finally got to the baseball field. Sissy had to go to her game, but she said she'd be back in time to see the end of my game. "Hi," I said. I warmed up with Brendan. Warmed up means you get your arm warm, and to do that you have to throw the ball. Finally, it was game time! I was up to bat fourth, and boy did I wallop the ball! I think wallop means you spank it or something. I got a triple on that, scoring two runners! Plus, after the fourth inning I caught a ball when I was playing shortstop! I just stuck my glove in the air, WHOP! the ball landed in my glove! We won that game, 8 to 5. Dad congratulated me and the team and then we went home. I had promised Yukon I would tell him all about it.

Sometimes kids just don't get lucky. Like that time I lost my bouncy ball under the stove (don't ask) and I never found it again. Or that time

I had to get stitches when I fell. Neither of those times were lucky. But how could I get so unlucky as to play catcher in a baseball game?! After I made the final out of the inning at first base, fielding a ground ball, Dad came up and said, "Rea, you aren't batting this inning, so come with me and I'll help you put your catcher's gear on." Well, I just about went bazonkers! Catcher! No way. I tried to protest, but Dad told me every kid had to play every position on the field. *Well,* I thought, *at least you get a ball come to you every pitch.* I could hear Sissy and Mom laughing when I went out to play catcher, but I didn't care. I loved making people laugh. Luckily, we do coach pitch, so the ball doesn't come as fast. But, as I soon found out, it hit the ground and then bounced up! I did everything I could to dodge the ball, because after all, we are Dodgers. I would jump up out of my crouched position every time the ball was pitched. Later, Sissy told me that the catcher was, believe it or not, actually supposed to catch the ball, instead of the umpire. Well, that confused me, because Ben and Landon and Rhett, the other catchers, just let the ball roll, so the umpire always got it and threw it back to the pitcher. Catcher is the worst position in baseball. I didn't enjoy wearing all of the catcher stuff and found it hard to move in it but I guess we have to try each position in order to know what we like to play. Boy, did I learn that being the catcher was not exactly my thing.

I think my first ball game was "A-Okay" from the high fives I received, mixed in with a few hugs from Mom and Dad. Sissy just said, "good game, Bro" and kinda slapped me on the shoulder. I guess that was good coming from a sister who is also playing softball on an opposite field and really not too concerned about my details. Our games nearly always were played at the same time so Mom walked back and forth between the two fields. Sometimes she missed my good hits or catches but we always (my Dad and I) enjoyed telling her and Sissy about my game and Sissy would fill us in on hers. It wasn't exactly family togetherness, but the best we could do under those circumstances I guess. At least Mom got her exercise too.

My grandparents in Alabama were very interested in my games and how they went. At the end of each one, I phoned them to give them my statistics—hits, runs, etc. The most exciting thing was when I got the game ball! I loved that part so much! It was signed by my coach with the date and what team we played. From then on, before every game, I told my coaches about being catcher and explained that being a catcher was NOT my favorite thing. Maybe I would be sent back out to the outfield or short stop in the next game. We have our second practice in two days so I can't wait to hit the ball and catch a few, if they are hit in my direction. I think I'm really into this baseball stuff.

My second practice went well. Sis decided she wanted to help with my team, so she ran the bases, played infield, played catcher, whatever Coach asked her to do. One time, Mark kept hitting the ball over to second base, the position she was playing, and she kept tagging me out! I never wanted her to help again. But she did, and no balls were hit to her in our scrimmage, so I guess it's OK. In my next game, I went 3 for 4, striking out once. I didn't feel very excited about that situation, but Sissy struck out a lot more than me. (No offense to her). It was our fourth game when disaster struck. I didn't see everything because I was goofing around with Will and Adam, but Dad and Sissy filled me in on the details later. Apparently, Collin had this really good hit that went all the way to centerfield! It was like a double or a triple or something, but the point is, that was a really good hit, so- (Sissy says I should get back to the real subject, because it's way more important than a good hit. I don't think so, but I'll go on anyway.) So, what happened was Mark was on second base, and boy did he run when Collin walloped that ball! The centerfielder relayed the ball to the second baseman who threw it home to try to get Mark out. Well, Sissy said Rhett was coming up to get ready to hit because he was up next. He looked up, just as the ball was thrown home. The ball hit him right under the left eye. He felt like he had been shot and started screaming. The coaches started crowding around him, and Dad said it was

like he was getting surgery or something. Everyone on the other team and me and Will and everyone else in the dugout came out and took a knee. "Taking a knee" is how you show respect to someone who's hurt. After that I said, "He deserves free ice cream!" Well, one good thing came out of that. Mark scored.

Now I think it's time to add a little spice to my story. After my fifth game, when I was 5 for 5 at the plate, this girl who looked to be about 9 or 10 rang our doorbell. She explained to Mom and Dad that she was the interviewer for her school newspaper. Her name was Sophie. She said she had been to all of my team's games and thought I was by far the best player on the team. I had to agree. So, she interviewed me for about 20 minutes. Most of the questions were pretty easy, like what's your favorite position to play, how long have you been playing, and who's your best friend on the team. But the last question caught me by surprise. "Do you hope to someday play in the major leagues?" I hadn't thought much about what I wanted to do when I grew up, so I didn't know how to answer her. Last I checked, Mom and Dad and Sissy told me I wanted to be a violin player and a firefighter. I thought about this for a while, because after all, I did have Michael Young's number. He plays for the Texas Rangers, and is number 10. After I considered all this, I took a deep breath and answered Sophie.

"Well Sophie, I've never really been interviewed before so I don't know how important my answers are, but I guess I also never thought about what I REALLY want to be when I grow up. I think playing the violin might be fun and being a firefighter would be good, but being a big baseball player might be more fun and maybe, who knows, I might be all three. I guess I could always change my mind, couldn't I?" Sophie replied that she didn't have all the answers either but that sounded good to her. After all, I remembered something my dentist told me recently when I mentioned that I got five hits and was up to bat just five times.

He said if I would be playing in the big leagues, I could be making a lot of money. I wonder if that's more than the dollar that I get for allowance. I think that would be good.

Sophie finished her interview and who knows what she'll do with it—just a waste of my time I guess but I like to make people happy so it wasn't so bad. By the time she prints it, no telling what I'll decide to do when I grow up! I might even tell Sissy that I want to play professional football because it has more excitement and reality. What is reality anyway?

"Hey family, what's up? I've been outside doing this silly interview or something like that for Sophie and beats me what she'll do with it. Did I miss dinner? Boy, this sports stuff beats me down." I thought about all the questions Sophie had asked

me and I was paying special attention to what I wanted to be when I grew up. Before I had decided for sure, Sissy called me down to dinner. We were having hotdogs, my favorite. I gobbled it up like a turkey.

I had my last regular season game that following Saturday. If we won, we would go to playoffs and have a chance to win the championship, but if we lost, we would be out. I was a little nervous and as usual, Sissy was packing my bat bag and complaining. "Why do I have to pack this? It's not my game." She kept saying. I just ignored her. I had more important things to worry about. When it finally came time for my game to begin, I was ready. We were playing the Cubs, a tough team.

After the second inning, the score was 9 to 1; they were winning, and it looked like we were gonna lose. But, we came up with an incredible comeback. We were winning, 12 to 11, going into the 5th inning. We got the first two outs right off the bat, (get it? *The bat*?) and then a ball was hit to me, at first base. It was a grounder, and I stopped it, but I couldn't pick it up. By the time I finally got it in my hand, the runner was safe. They got four runs before we finally got the third out. I hoped my error hadn't cost us the game! I got a hit with one out, and Ethan hit the winning hit, and Adam scored the winning run. We won 16 to 15. The parents started jumping up and screaming and raising their arms. At first, I don't think we all realized we had won, but

when Dad came over and gave me a high five, I knew we had beaten the mighty Cubs. I ran screaming out of the dugout and throwing my hat all around. Collin tackled Brendan, and I grabbed Will in a big bear hug. We had won! We were going to the playoffs! That was by far the most exciting game I had ever played.

A few days later, I was getting ready for our playoff game. We were playing the Indians, a team that had gone undefeated all season long. I was pretty nervous. Sissy didn't get to see my game because she had two softball games that day, but that didn't stop me or my team! Actually, it did. Even though I had 3 hits to my credit, we still lost 20 to 6. So we weren't the Little League champions, but we did come in 3rd place. I was a little disappointed, but you can't have everything. Sissy came in 4th place in her league, and she had gotten 3 hits in those 2 games. I got the game ball again, and it felt great. I really do love baseball, and I think I've decided what I want to be when I grow up. I'm thinking, a Texas Rangers baseball player, and on Sundays after church I'll be playing for the Dallas Cowboys.

That following Monday, I got an email from Sophie with her school newspaper attached.

REAGAN HAWKINS FROM DODGERS HELPS TEAM PLACE #3

Reagan Hawkins, #10 from the Little League Dodgers had an incredible game against the mighty Indians, an undefeated team. He got 3 hits, a single and two doubles. The writers from Johnson Elementary School are electing Hawkins as the most talented Little League baseball player.

-Sophie Ortiz

I jumped with joy! I was the most talented Little League baseball player. Maybe I'll grow up to be just a baseball player. After all, I seem to be better at it, and I think it has a little bit more reality. (I still don't know what that word means). I can't wait until next year!

Larry the Ant and His Adventures

Holy moley! What's all that noise? Larry the ant lifted one eyelid slightly to see what was making all that noise. YIKES! Some kind of monster was right in front of him. Larry opened both eyes fully to see his boss right in front of his face. The boss was yelling something at Larry and his face was red and he looked really mad. "Get up, you lazy ant. All you ever do is goof off!" the boss said.

Larry yawned, stretched and jumped out of bed. "Is it morning already?" Larry asked. He knew it was really morning because he could see all the other ant workers scurrying back and forth doing their chores.

"Yes, it's morning. It's way past morning. Now get busy!" the boss roared. Larry ran to his work station before the boss could say anything else.

Just before Larry got to his work station he remembered that he forgot to go to the cafeteria for his morning meal, but Larry was not about to do anything else to make the boss mad. He looked at the work schedule to see what he was supposed to do today. "Aww man!" he said to himself. Today, his assignment was to carry eggs from the queen's

nursery up to the top of the nest so the eggs could be warmed by the sun's heat. "Same old thing every day!" he said to himself. Larry had been doing this job every day this week. Actually, he had been doing it every day for as long as he could remember. Then he reminded himself that one day he had been assigned to go outside to help bring in some food that had been found by one of the outside scouts. The thought of that food made him think about how hungry he was. Maybe he could think of a way to go by the cafeteria on the way back from one of his trips.

Larry slowly wiped his eyes so he could wake up and start moving, and he decided to detour by the cafeteria anyway. To his dismay, there was nothing in sight for a quick snack so he decided he had to get to work. Maybe he would forget his hunger or just maybe find a bite of food dropped by another worker.

"Hey, Larry! I need help carrying these eggs. Could you give me a hand?" Anthony, Larry's best friend, called from the top of the staircase." "Sure, Anthony, be right there," Larry called back to his friend. "Easy now," Larry told Anthony as they hobbled down the stairs. "To the left. There, we made it." "Thanks, Lare. The queen still has about a hundred more eggs to bring into the sun. Guess we better get busy." "Yeah, I guess," Larry mumbled. "Hey, man, what's the matter?" Anthony asked. "I just don't like doing the same job every

day," Larry said. "I wish I could have some variety, you know, like your brother." "My brother is thirteen. He's a whole lot busier than I am. The boss lets ants twelve and under do just one job a day. Once you're thirteen, you start going out to get food, something extremely dangerous. I'm glad I'm only ten." Anthony told Larry. "Well, I'm not. Where does your brother sign in every morning to get food?" Larry inquired. "Over there," Anthony said, pointing to the doors right outside the cafeteria. "But don't get any ideas, Larry. All those ants go to get food from picnickers, who are humans. Thousands of ants get squashed every day while trying to get food." "I know," Larry grumbled. "You go on up, Anthony. I'll be right there."

"Where is Johnny?" Larry overheard the head food ant ask the group. No one answered. "Oh, well. I guess we'll have to go an ant short today. Everybody, in line." Larry grinned mischievously to himself. He then checked behind his shoulder to make sure the adults and Anthony weren't looking. They were all busy, so Larry scampered over to the food line. "Here, boss!" he said to the head ant. "Sorry I'm late." "Hello, Johnny, I'm glad you're here," he said, thinking Larry was Johnny. "Alright, troops, let's head out, shall we?" The food ants gave a big whoop, and then they all, including Larry, headed outside.

"I wonder how far we have to go," mumbled Larry, because he was already getting tired, but he didn't dare complain to the head food ant. The tall grass seemed like a forest to the tiny ant legs and sometimes they had to detour around heavy bushes or shrubs along the way. The food ant line seemed to go forever with everyone in a straight line and marching along like an army. None would dare stop to munch along the way or else they might get left and the boss ant would really be upset if one went missing. Since this was Larry's first mission on the food line, he really didn't know what to expect, so he decided to try and find out without anyone learning his secret. "Boy do I wish I had eaten today," exclaimed Larry as they rounded a big opening in the grass.

Larry decided he must watch the other ants, so he could follow and learn what their job would be. Up ahead, he could see that there was little or no grass and he could see groups of humans, some sitting on the ground and others walking around. He figured that these must be picnickers and food might be close by. He checked out Anthony's brother and stayed close to him, just hoping he wouldn't get squashed.

Back in the anthill, Anthony was searching for Larry to help him carry more eggs up to the sunshine. He searched in every corner and called out to him but couldn't find him. Finally, he gave up and asked William, his friend, to help carry the

loads. “William, will you help me carry the eggs up to the sunshine?” asked Anthony. “Sure, man,” replied William. “I have to do this job sometimes too so I don't mind, but where is Larry?” he asked. “I can't find him but I'm sure he has another job to do and we can catch up with him later,” said Anthony.

Larry was getting frightened. The line was getting closer and closer to humans. “Alright, men,” the head ant said.“You know where to go. Get your partner, and get your assigned food.” “I’m sorry to bother you, boss, but who is my partner?” Larry asked. “Brad, over there,” the boss answered, pointing to Anthony’s brother. “Now please remember your partner!” “Yes sir,” Larry replied and then walked over to Brad. Brad pulled him aside. “Look, Larry, I know you’re my kid brother’s best friend. What are you doing here?” he whispered. “I am sick and tired of carrying the queen’s eggs out to the sunlight every single day, so I snuck into this line.” “Listen, Larry. I would give anything to do your job. I am worried every day before I go out. I don’t know if I’ll come back alive!” Brad hissed at Larry. “I’m sorry. I didn’t know!” Larry cried. “Well, you can’t go back now without Mr. Antwoin seeing you. Come with me and hope you come back alive.” Brad said, leading Larry through the picnickers. “Grab that cheese,” Brad instructed him. Brad grabbed a crumb of white cheese himself. Larry was so scared, he was

trembling. If a human saw him, they would squash him for sure.

Back at the anthill, Anthony was getting worried. Where had Larry gone? He had searched everywhere he could think of for his friend, but Larry seemed to have disappeared. "Larry!" he called from the basement. No answer. Then, a horrible thought struck him. *What if Larry went into the food line, and was outside this second? He could die!* Anthony thought. *I have to save him!* Anthony put on his jacket and hurried outside to rescue his friend.

"Geez! Where in the world do I start looking for Larry in this big space?" shouted Anthony. He shook with fear and excitement as he pondered where to start looking, and he knew he could not ask for help because that would surely get Larry into trouble. He paced in circles trying to decide what to do and when he couldn't think of anything else, he started walking slowly away from his home just hoping to get an idea as he walked. It seemed hours since he left his anthill, and it was getting late, but he couldn't stop yet. He tried calling-- "Larry, Larry, where are you?" but didn't hear any noises. He kept walking in circles trying to remember his route so he wouldn't get lost.

William had stopped to rest before going into the kitchen to help prepare supper, and wondered where Anthony had disappeared to, but didn't have time to look for him.

Brad kept his eye on Larry for a couple of reasons. He was trying to protect him from the adults and being squashed and also protecting himself as he figured it would be more difficult to squash two ants than one. He was staying close to Larry and leading him around the picnic area. Their little legs walked very fast but it took a long time to maneuver around the people and ALL that food. They managed to get to the white cheese but just as they were about to get a crumb, some humans walked over and their feet were so-o-o-o close to Larry and Brad so they had to hide under a blade of grass. It seemed like everyone in the food line had scattered and they were hard to locate because they, too, were trying to stay safe. "Larry, let's play it cool for awhile and look around for another picnic where there might be fewer humans," suggested Brad. "Okay Brad, that sounds great. I'm sorry I've come, and I wish I'd just stayed home," replied Larry. "Good choice," Brad mumbled quietly.

Larry was startled out of his thoughts as he heard a little girl scream. "Mommy, Mommy, there's an ant!" she yelled from the top of her lungs. "Hurry, Larry, we have to get out of here!" Brad yelled, though those words didn't need to be said, for Larry was already way ahead of Brad. Suddenly, they both heard the ground shake as an angry father chased after them. Brad and Larry scurried as fast as they could away from him. Quickly, they dove behind a large oak tree. The father ran past them.

"Whew, was that close." Larry was breathing hard. "Maybe I should take you back home," Brad said, looking at Larry. "Maybe," Larry agreed. "Thanks a lot, Brad. I'm sorry about all this." "Don't worry about it. Just next time, wait until you're old enough to join the food line," Brad told him. They walked back towards the anthill, continuously looking behind their shoulders to see if the angry father was still chasing them. Larry would never forget the picnic that day. Sure, there was food everywhere, perfect for little ants, but there were also dangerous humans, giant ones at that, and little tattletale girls who hated ants. *Anthony was right,* Larry thought. He stopped. *Anthony! I completely forgot about him! He's probably worried sick about me!* Larry, rushing, told Brad about him and Anthony. "I have to go find him!" he finished. "It doesn't take a genius to realize I snuck out into the food line! Bye, Brad. And thanks!" Larry called as he scurried to the anthill, leaving Brad all to himself thinking, *What a strange little ant. I wish I'd had a friend like that when I was 10.*

Larry started his long walk back to the anthill alone, feeling lonely, scared, cold, and still very hungry. He actually didn't remember the walk to the picnic area being so long and as he walked, he started feeling very sorry for trying to handle this job before he was assigned to it. He was especially upset that he had left his best friend, Anthony, to do his original job of caring for the Queen's eggs. "If only I

had listened to Anthony and not acted selfishly," cried Larry. He had no idea that Anthony was searching for him at this very moment. As he walked, he started to feel that he wasn't sure which direction to go so this made him even more scared. After walking for several hours, he stopped to rest, and then he knew he was lost so he wondered what in the world he would do now.

Suddenly, he had an idea! Maybe he could look for another picnic area and find a few morsels of food as he searched for the way back. So off he went again! He walked a little bit and stopped and listened for human voices, and finally he began to hear something that sounded familiar---YES!!! some children playing. "Great, great—what a wonderful thing to hear!" said Larry as his ears perked up and he continued to walk toward the voices. He still had a long distance to walk but he headed in that direction, hoping.

Meanwhile, Anthony started on his journey to find Larry. He still didn't know which direction to go and he couldn't remember if anyone had ever said where they went to the picnic area, so he just had to decide himself. Being the smart fellow he was, he looked at the grass all around the anthill for something that looked like a path made by many ants going in a straight line and WOW there it was right before his eyes! "Larry, Larry, I am going to find you before you get squashed—just you wait and see!" breathed Anthony.

Larry ran as fast as his little legs would carry him through the grass to where he heard the children playing. He saw two boys tossing a football, a girl and a boy playing Frisbee, and four girls dancing around in a circle. *Hooray!* Larry thought happily as he scampered past them to the food ants. He couldn't find them! They were gone, at least until dinnertime. "Brad! Brad! Mr. Antwoin!" he called, but it was no use. They weren't anywhere around. Suddenly, Larry heard a rustle in the bushes. "H-h-hello?" Larry said weakly. He was scared. Could a human be behind the bushes? "Hi, I'm Beatrice," said a voice. A bee's head popped out from behind the bushes. "What are you doing here, little ant?" Beatrice asked Larry. "I'm lost," Larry replied. "I was out here gathering food, and when I tried to get back to my anthill, I went in circles." "Well, I have to gather pollen now, but after I'm done I can help you get back to your home," Beatrice told Larry. "Thanks a lot, Beatrice!" Larry said joyfully. "Do you want me to wait here until you're done?" he asked Beatrice. "No," Beatrice answered, sounding very surprised. "You can come with me." "Great!" Larry replied. "I've always wanted to fly!" And with that, Beatrice picked Larry up with her legs and jumped into the air.

"Larry! Larry!" Anthony called from the picnic area. He had just arrived at the place where the ant tracks had led him. It was 5:00 o'clock, only

an hour until suppertime, so he could wait for the food ants to come and then ask them about Larry. "But I don't want to wait an hour," Anthony said to himself. "Besides, it will be getting dark soon." So Anthony kept crawling through the picnic area. There were only about 4 families there. Suddenly, Anthony saw something that just might solve the mystery of Larry's disappearance. "A piece of cheese!" Anthony said to himself. Anthony followed the track probably left by Larry, but after about 9 paces, the tracks stopped. "Something must have happened to him here," Anthony said as the horrible thought struck him. "I have to find out what happened, and fast!" Anthony spoke with determination.

"Well, gee whiz, where in the world would Larry have gone from here if he had to leave in a hurry?" Anthony pondered. He searched all around for more cheese or tracks of any kind. He even crawled up to the top of some grass blades and looked as far as he could; and when he didn't get any hints or see anything to help him, he sat down to think. *If I were Larry, where would I go?* thought Anthony. Then he had the same idea as Larry about finding another picnic area where the food ants might be, so great minds think alike!

Anthony started out trying to be careful and look for more clues as he walked. As he seriously looked, he noticed that the grass was separated in places as if either ants or humans might have passed

by that way. He decided to follow that trail for awhile. There were no more crumbs, so Anthony decided that Larry would not have travelled back that way with food for the anthill. Then he became more scared that Larry was in trouble. "Oh, where do I look now?" cried Anthony. "I hope that I can find Larry and then that we can find our way back home," he said as he became very frustrated.

Beatrice and Larry were flying back to the anthill. "Wow, from the air, everything looks so big and different. Where are we?" cried Larry. Beatrice was having trouble getting enough pollen and could not return without the proper amount, so when she found her sources, she dipped down to the earth from the air, set Larry down on some grass and proceeded to gather her pollen. "Beatrice, please don't lose me and leave me here because I would be lost forever!" begged Larry. "Don't worry, Larry," Beatrice comforted him. "I have to go to a field with very tall flowers; some are even in a tree. I don't want to leave you there, because you might get lost under all the shrubs on the ground. I'll come pick you up when I'm finished, which will be in about 20 minutes," she told him as she flew off into the sky. He was still very nervous about the terrible situation though but tried to sit quietly and patiently while Beatrice did her work. His hunger grew steadily but he just had to put that aside for now.

Finally, Anthony arrived at the other picnic area where the children were playing and he was so

happy! "There is hope here, because Larry had to find some more food. I'm sure he is around some place, but where, where, where?" sighed Anthony. *Oh, how I wish I had longer legs and could see over the tall grass, but in the meantime, I will just walk back and forth and hopefully will bump right into Larry,* he thought. Suddenly, he heard some buzzing over in the wild flowers and stopped to listen. A bee buzzed over near Anthony and said, "Hello, my name is Buster. I am gathering pollen to take back to my beehive." Anthony felt a little better just having someone to talk to, so he explained that his best friend Larry had gone in the ant food line and he was searching for him because he knew Larry was lost. Buster agreed to help him search for Larry, and would carry him through the air which sounded exciting to Anthony. He had never flown before and for the next minute or so, he felt less tense about his journey alone.

"This is your beehive?" Anthony asked full of curious excitement. In front of him was a beautiful, yellow house that had to have at least 100 bee workers carrying pollen, honey, and baby bees. It was an awesome sight to behold! *I wonder if visitors to our anthill think the same thing when they see us*, Anthony thought. "This is it," Buster said. "Hey Barbara!" Buster yelled, calling a girl bee over. "Anthony here is looking for his friend Larry. Have you seen any other ants around here?" "No, I'm sorry, Buster. Have you seen Bea? I can't find her

anywhere. She should have been back here about 10 minutes ago." Barbara informed Buster. "No, sorry. But while Anthony and I are looking for Larry, we'll keep an eye out for Bea," Buster assured Barbara. "Thanks, and good luck finding your friend!" Barbara called to Anthony as she buzzed away. "Alright, hop on, buddy," Buster said to Anthony. "Let's go." Off they went, through the sky, all of the humans looking like, well, ants! Anthony loved the feeling of the wind in his face, blowing his legs crazily. *Ah, this is the life,* he thought to himself. *Now if only I could find Larry.*

Back on the ground, Larry kept pacing back and forth. Where was Beatrice? *She should be here by now, shouldn't she? H*e thought to himself. Suddenly, Larry felt the ground shake. A little boy was coming right at him! "Hi, little ant," he said gently to Larry. "Don't worry, I won't hurt you." Then the boy whipped out a glass case, and before Larry could even think to run away, the boy grabbed him and shoved him in the case with 3 other ants. "This will be great for my collection for school!" the boy said as he skipped away to show his parents. "Oh no. Oh no, oh no, oh!" Larry yelled, banging on the case. "I have to get out of here!" "It's okay," one ant said, trying to calm him down. "What!" Larry snapped. "I'm trapped in a case! How can it be okay?" "I'm Kenneth," the ant said. "And this is Adam and Sophie." "Great," Larry said, worriedly. "Nice to meet you. Now how do we get out of

here?" "Relax," Adam said calmly. "Before you came, Sophie thought of a plan. Sophie, do you mind repeating it?" "Sure" said Sophie. "By the way, what were you doing out there before you were caught and dumped in here with us?" Larry explained how he had been working in the food brigade when he was surprised by the human kids and chased away from the group, and how he had been helped by the bees. The way he told it, it sounded like things like that happened to him all the time but he didn't mention the small fact that he wasn't even supposed to be out of the anthill. That could wait until another time. "But enough about me," said Larry. "I want to hear about the plan you have to get us out of here and back home. It's getting dark out there!" "Okay," said Sophie. "Here's what I had in mind. First of all, I don't want to talk too loud because we don't want the boy to hear us and a good plan is hard to think up. Before this boy gets too far, we have to act fast. We don't want to. . . . . .

"I sure hope you all have talked this out," said Larry, "because it sounds kind of like a plan I once saw in a movie and it didn't work." "Well," Adam said, "it sounded like that to me also, but I remembered that in the movie they made the mistake of not thinking about their surroundings and by not using everything they had at their disposal to help in their escape. Listen to this! Where are we? What are we in? This is a glass case, right? We don't have any tools. Just us. Here's what we need to do. Larry,

what's around us?" Larry shrugged. "Grass and sticks and trees. Why?" "Because," Kenneth chipped in, "That will help us with our plan. Sophie, help us escape!"

Back in the sky, Anthony had just dropped to the ground in a forest. "This is the route I take every day to get the best pollen," Buster explained. "Wait here. Bea might be in this forest gathering pollen, too." And with that, Buster flew into the sky again. Anthony looked at the sky. "It looks like it's about 6:00. Oh, where is Larry?" he said to himself. In about 5 minutes, Buster flew back down again, this time with another bee. "Anthony, this is Beatrice, or Bea, and Bea, this is Anthony. Bea says she helped Larry, but when she came back, he was gone!" Buster explained to Anthony. "Oh no! This is exactly what I thought would happen! He's gone forever!" Anthony exclaimed with agony. "It's OK, Anthony. He couldn't have gone far. He's just a tiny ant," Bea assured him. "Let's look around. He must be here somewhere."

Kenneth had just hopped out of the glass case when the little boy came back to get it. The four ants dove behind a large tree just in time. "Where are my ants?" the little boy cried, shaking the case around. "They're gone! Mommy! Daddy!" he shouted, running back to the picnic area. The ants did a dance and high fived each other. "Sophie, that was an awesome idea! Adam, it was great how we all lifted you up and you got a stick

to push the top off! You have got to be the strongest ant in the world!" Larry exclaimed. They all laughed. "Well, now for the important part, Larry," Sophie said seriously. "We need to get you back to your home." "Yes," Larry agreed. "Come on, let's walk around a little until that little boy goes home." The ants started walking. Suddenly, Larry heard a buzzing sound above his head. "Beatrice?" he said, hoping it was his bee friend. Then, all at once, something fell from the sky. It landed on a pile of leaves next to the four ants. "Larry!" the voice shouted, jumping up. "Who are you?" Larry asked, backing up. "Anthony!" the voice said, shaking leaves off of his body. "Oh, Anthony!" the two ants ran to each other and hugged. "I'm so happy to see you!" Anthony told Larry. "Hey Buster, Beatrice! Come here!" Two bees flew down and landed by all the ant friends. "You must be Larry," Buster said. "The ant Anthony has been looking for." "I am, and thank you for helping him!" Larry said, figuring that Buster was Anthony's friend. "Hi, Beatrice!" Larry greeted his friend. "Hi, Larry. I'm glad you're safe. Let's all walk home together." Beatrice said as they walked.

"Yeah, I have to get home and tell William what happened. I left him doing our job!" Anthony told the group. "I hope you learned never to sneak into the food line again," Sophie told Larry. "Oh, I have," Larry assured her. "I sure learned my lesson!" "Well, let's get home, and you can tell us

all about your adventures and new friends," Buster suggested. "Oh, you won't believe the trouble I got into!" Larry said. "I would believe it!" Anthony said happily as the friends all laughed.

THE END

The Magical Harp

"And Hans Van Buren's magical harp was never seen again. Some people don't give up on the idea that it is in these Alabama woods, where, when Hans Van Buren was not playing for people's operas or concerts, he spent all his free time. Others believe that the famous harp vanished." Mrs. Nichols snapped her fingers, "just like that. And anyone who finds the harp will always have fame, fortune, and good luck, just like this well-known harpist."

The school bell shook the walls of Fosters Middle School, announcing loud and clear that it was three o'clock, the end of another tough school day for all the middle-schoolers. "Class dismissed," Mrs. Nichols told her eighth graders. "Have a wonderful weekend, and I'll see you all back here on Monday."

Thirteen- year- old Cody Thomas grabbed his history books and walked out of Mrs. Nichols' eighth-grade history class and to his locker. He hurriedly grabbed all of his other books and binders and stuffed them into his backpack. On his way to grab his pens and pencils, his arm bumped the locker shelf, sending all his writing utensils flying

through the air. Cody stomped his foot and thought angrily, *Why does it have to happen to me? Why am I the one who always has bad luck?* It was true. Cody Thomas has had horrible luck ever since he was four years old. Since then, he had never had a friend, and the townspeople living in Fosters never spoke to him. They didn't want to catch Cody's "bad luck disease." Some of his bad luck was small stuff, like his dropping his writing utensils. Others, like when Cody had first moved to Fosters, a small Alabama town near Birmingham, and had lost his teacher's prize horse that he had let Cody borrow over the weekend, were big. Cody hated having bad luck.

His teacher's words rang through his ears. "And anyone who finds the harp will have fame, fortune, and good luck, just like this well-known harpist." *If I could find that harp*, Cody thought, *I could have good luck, and I could finally have a friend.* So right then and there, Cody decided he would begin a great harp search the next day. He would start searching at the beginning of his father's property, a few miles from his house, and make his way up, back to his house. He biked home quickly so he could get some rest. It was going to be a busy weekend!

The next day, bright and early, after he had eaten breakfast and done his daily chores, Cody hopped on his bike to begin his "Great Harp Search". He left at about seven-thirty that morning,

deciding to take Striker, his German Shepherd, along for the adventure. After Cody had been pedaling for a long time, he stopped his bike to get a snack out for him and water for Striker. As he munched on his ham and cheese sandwich, he thought about what his life would be like if he found the harp. At first he didn't believe in the old harp story. How could a 100-year-old harp still be there after all the years of storms? Cody was sure animals would have been chewing on it or playing with it too. But lately Cody had been getting more and more desperate for good luck, so much so that he started to believe that Hans Van Buren's harp still existed. Cody put his trash in his backpack, ready to begin his journey again. Striker trailed behind him, panting and enjoying the run through the woods, even though it was a hot day, and not a cloud was in sight.

A little while later, when the sun was high in the sky, Cody stopped his bike and got off. This was as far as he had ever gone on his dad's property, so he decided to walk a little ways so he could get off his bike for a while. Striker ran ahead of Cody, determined to beat the boy to wherever they were going. After Striker had gone so far away from Cody that he could hardly see the dog, Cody heard Striker's low bark. Cody broke into a run, suddenly worried about his dog. He got there just in time to see a rabbit dart away, eager to get away from the dog. That was why Striker was barking, but Cody

was looking at something else. Cody stood staring open-mouthed at a lovely, golden, foot-and-a half - long harp. The harp was resting upright on a rock almost as big as Cody! The rock was sitting in a small body of water. Cody was slightly shocked at how small the instrument was. Nevertheless, this had to be Hans Van Buren's harp. How many other harps do you find in a forest? *So it's true,* Cody thought. *It's really true. It must be magical. How else could it still be here, golden and shiny, after one hundred years?* Cody was speechless. Finally, after he had stared at it for more than five minutes, he slowly walked toward it, avoiding the water by hopping on the rocks. When he got to the rock where the harp was sitting, he reached out and picked up the beautiful harp. He strummed the strings, and it made a heavenly noise. Cody, holding the harp, and Striker, wondering why he and his master had traveled all this way just to get a harp, both walked back to Cody's bike. Cody carefully set the harp in his backpack and started for home. He pedaled much more furiously to his house than he did from his house. He was eager to tell his family about his lucky find.

As soon as Cody got home, he gave his dog a big bowl of water, then went to find his family. "Mom! Dad! Kyle! Madelyn!" Cody called, addressing his mom, dad, brother, and sister. His mother was the first who came running, her curly brown hair flying. "Cody, you're back," she hugged

him. "Did you find what you were looking for?" Cody could tell that she didn't quite believe in the magical harp, but that didn't matter. It was right there in his backpack! "As a matter of fact, I did," Cody told her. "But I'd like to show the whole family at the same time." At that moment, Cody's sixteen-year-old brother, Kyle, ran into the room at the same time as Cody's father and eight-year-old sister, Madelyn, came tumbling down the stairs.

"Hey, man, we heard you calling. Anything wrong?" Kyle asked. "Wrong? Everything's fantastic!" Cody told his family, his blue eyes shining. "I found this harp. Hans Van Buren's magical harp to be exact. You know, the famous musician from Holland who moved to Alabama? I found it in the woods." Cody removed the golden harp from his backpack. His family gasped. "It's beautiful," Madelyn whispered. Cody nodded. "It's supposed to bring good luck to anyone who finds it. I'm hoping it will bring luck to me." "Wow, son. That's quite a find," his father told him, examining the harp. "You better put that in a safe spot." Cody agreed. "Oh, I will, Dad." "Where did you find it?" Mrs. Thomas asked Cody. "Sitting on a rock by a riverbank a few miles from here," Cody answered. "Great job, son. Why don't you go get some rest?" Mr. Thomas suggested. "You must be very tired." "I am," Cody replied. "See you, guys!" "Bye, Cody! Great find!" Kyle told Cody.

"Thanks," Cody answered. He walked upstairs to his room, feeling very proud of himself. He couldn't wait for school to start Monday. Maybe he could finally have a friend!

*** *** *** *** *** *** *** *** *** *** *** ***

When Cody biked to school on Monday, he felt like he was a celebrity! The townspeople were swarming on him, and every boy at school wanted to be his best friend! Cody kept the harp in his backpack, and tried to watch it the whole day. It was kind of hard to do that when everyone was swarming all over him. Cody really enjoyed all the attention he was getting. He also didn't have any bad luck. Finally, he had friends! Finally, everyone talked to him!

A few days later when Cody was about to bike to school, he looked in his closet to get his harp, just like every day, but this time it wasn't there! Cody was shocked! He knew he had put it in his closet the night before! But there was no time to look now. He'd be late for school. As he biked to his school, he knew something **was** wrong. No one was surrounding him! Everyone gave him the cold looks they had given him **before** he had found the harp. At school, no one was his friend, either. Then, at lunchtime, Cody began to figure it all out. Everyone was just pretending to be his friend because somehow they had heard he had found the magical harp. Of course! Why hadn't he realized that

before? But who could have told them that he had discovered the harp? Cody thought for a minute, and then the idea dawned on him. His eight-year-old sister, Madelyn, must have told everyone! And if his hunch was correct, when he picked her up from her third grade class, everyone would be swarming over her, because her big mouth told everyone that she had the harp!

Sure enough, when Cody got off his bike and headed to pick his sister up, Madelyn had dozens of girls all over her! She had more friends than Cody had seen her with before.

Cody knew she was the culprit, so he would talk to her when they got home. When they got home, before Madelyn hopped off her bike to go do homework, Cody stopped her. "Madelyn," he started. "Did you take the harp I found in the woods?" After a slight hesitation, Madelyn admitted that she had. "It was so pretty," she told her older brother. "Madelyn, that was wrong," Cody told her. "I know. I'm sorry, Cody. Here, you can have it back."

"Even though taking it was wrong, I don't want it. You can keep it if you want, but I don't want to have anything to do with it," Cody told Madelyn. "And, Madelyn, unless you want fake friends, don't keep it, because all those girls are just pretending to be your pals." "I don't want it," Madelyn said. "What should I do with it?" "Just put it in the attic. We shouldn't throw a beauty like

that in the garbage," Cody told her. Madelyn apologized again, and went to go put the harp in the attic. Cody stayed behind, smiling to himself, wondering what the next school day would bring.

****

The next day was the same as before. Cody didn't have any "friends." But that was okay with Cody. The night before he had decided that if he didn't have real friends, then he didn't want any friends at all. But Cody didn't end the day without a friend. He had just swung his leg around his bike ready to go home, when a boy about Cody's age ran from the school shouting, "Wait, Cody, wait!" Cody almost fell over. Was a boy really asking him to wait? Cody couldn't believe it. Nevertheless, Cody waited. When the boy finally got to Cody, he said without hesitation, "Cody, will you be my friend?" This time Cody did fall off his bike. He recovered himself quickly, however, then asked the boy, "Why do you want to be my friend?" The boy looked ashamed and said, "Well I was one of those boys who was pretending to be your friend at first, when I heard you found Hans Van Buren's harp. Then, later, I decided I really did like you. You didn't act all snobbish like most kids would if they got all that attention," the boy explained. "So, can I be your friend? My name's Spencer, by the way," Spencer told Cody.

Cody grinned, held out his hand, and said, "Spencer, when I was in bed last night, dreaming of how nice it would be to have a friend, you were the kind of friend I wanted." This time Spencer smiled and shook Cody's outstretched hand. "Thanks, man," he said. "Want to go for a bike ride together?" Cody agreed, and the two best friends had a blast. Spencer and Cody are still great friends today, and they will always remain that way. As for Cody, well, he decided that he only had bad luck because he didn't have any confidence in himself. And now that he has a friend like Spencer, he doesn't have to worry about not having confidence.

Years later, when Cody was grown up and had a son of his own, he was helping his parents clean out their house. They had decided that the large house was just too much for them, and they were to move the next week.

Cody's thirteen-year-old son, Jake, was helping his father clean out the attic. When almost everything was put into the moving van, Jake pulled out an old, dusty harp from behind a large chest. Jake wiped off the cobwebs and dust, admiring the instrument. With wonder he asked, "Hey Dad, what's this?"

The End

Printed in the United States
213669BV00003B/2/P

9 780981 919560

44197919R00114

Made in the USA
Charleston, SC
16 July 2015